BRIGHT NOTES

THE MAJOR WORKS BY JEAN-PAUL SARTRE

Intelligent Education

INFLUENCE PUBLISHERS

Nashville, Tennessee

BRIGHT NOTES: Major Works

www.BrightNotes.com

No part of this publication may be used or reproduced in any manner whatsoever without written permission, except in the case of brief quotations in critical articles and reviews. For permissions, contact Influence Publishers http://www.influencepublishers.com.

ISBN: 978-1-645422-64-8 (Paperback)
ISBN: 978-1-645422-65-5 (eBook)

Published in accordance with the U.S. Copyright Office Orphan Works and Mass Digitization report of the register of copyrights, June 2015.

Originally published by Monarch Press.
Connor P. Hartnett, 1965
2020 Edition published by Influence Publishers.

Interior design by Lapiz Digital Services. Cover Design by Thinkpen Designs.

Printed in the United States of America.

Library of Congress Cataloging-in-Publication Data forthcoming.
Names: Intelligent Education
Title: BRIGHT NOTES: Major Works
Subject: STU004000 STUDY AIDS / Book Notes

CONTENTS

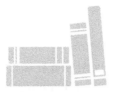

INTRODUCTION TO JEAN-PAUL SARTRE

Sartre has probably exercised a greater impact upon the intellectual life of Europe since the Second World War than any other man of letters. He has made a vogue and battle cry out of an abstruse philosophical doctrine; his works have been translated into all civilized tongues and a library has been written about his personality and production; he has become a legend in his lifetime, an oracle to some, a spokesman of the devil to others. In order to understand his books better, we must first acquaint ourselves with the relevant biographical data preceding and concurrent with his literary development.

CHILDHOOD

Jean-Paul Sartre was born in Paris on June 21, 1905. His family was solidly upper-middle class, that is, they belonged to the segment of French society that has forged the military, political and economic might of the country and formulated its ethical standards for the last century and a half. His father died in Indo-China when Jean-Paul was only two years old. The child was brought up by his mother and maternal grandparents. The grandfather, Professor Schweitzer of the Sorbonne, adored Jean-Paul and provided him with all that could foster his intellectual development. The child showed an early aptitude to literary expression. In fact, in this milieu it was inconceivable to be no better than mediocre: Dr. Schweitzer made it clear from the outset that great things were expected of Jean-Paul. The boy accepted the standards of excellence imposed upon him by his grandfather. In his long critique of Genet, Sartre was to come to the conclusion that talent is a decision. Talent was certainly a decision young Sartre made. He was not a "gifted child" by standards of intelligence tests. Good was always rewarded in the Schweitzer household, and all evil punished.

The perfection of the moral order during his sheltered childhood (he was not sent to school until he was much older) must have given the sensitive adolescent one of his keenest disappointments when he came to realize that the same rules did not govern society as a whole. The sense of indignation he felt will be perceptible in the bulk of the author's literary production. In turn, it will make him resentful of the family environment that had presented a falsified version of the world, even though this may have been done out of affection for him.

In 1916 Mme. Sartre remarried. This marks a turning point in Jean-Paul's life. His stepfather, a high-ranking officer, appears to have been a stern, military type, a staggering change from Dr. Schweitzer's genteel intellectuality. To make matters worse, Jean-Paul was now far from being the center of his mother's existence. She was trying to adjust to her husband's way of living. Young Sartre felt unwanted at their new home in provincial La Rochelle. A study of Sartre's fiction reveals a series of heroes whose basic existential experience has been a sense of superfluity inherited from early childhood: Orestes in *The Flies;* Goetz, an illegitimate child, in the *Devil and the Good Lord*; Philippe, a general's stepson, in *The Reprieve*. His two best-known essays, Baudelaire (significantly, Baudelaire was also the stepson of a general) and *On Genet* are likewise built on the proposition that these men had an awareness of being supernumeraries since the dawn of their existence. Discounting some incidental details, these last two works are probably the best autobiographical works Sartre has written. Sartre's revolt against society and even against creation in general originates from this period. We cannot fail to notice that he intensely detests people who believe that they have their places under the sun assigned by God, who feel at home and self-confident in their milieu, while disputing the right of others to exist. Sartre visualized himself as an out-person when he was still very young. He has not tried to sublimate this awareness by hating in turn those who are outcasts of an even "lower" order than himself; nor has he attempted to gain admittance to the in-group by abject adulation.

Sartre attended the lycée of La Rochelle until 1919, when the family moved back to Paris. The hours spent away from the home did not mitigate the tension either. He had been exposed to the school environment without sufficient preparation: the legend of superiority, nurtured by the grandparents, was now to be shattered. Jean-Paul was short and suffered from a severe case of astigmatism. One is tempted to infer that many of his later ontological tenets were the result of a personal psychological condition. Sartre maintains that all evil is projection. The acute awareness of the contingency, the unnecessary nature of the universe as experienced by the central figure in *Nausea* would certainly seem to be a projective response from someone who himself feel rejected; and this novel may be considered as a fictional corollary of Sartre's main philosophical contribution, *Being and Nothingness*.

TEACHING CAREER

Sartre passed the aggregation, the diploma that admits one to the teaching profession, in 1929, after one unsuccessful attempt a year earlier. He was assigned to the Lycée of Le Havre, where he taught philosophy from 1931 until 1933. Later that year he was granted a fellowship to study at the French Institute of Berlin. While in Berlin he did research under the guidance of Edmund Husserl, founder of the phenomenological method in philosophy. Husserl's theory profoundly affected Sartre's ideological outlook. He came back to France to teach two more years at Le Havre, then taught at Laon and finally at the Lycée Pasteur in Paris. He was drafted into the French army in 1939. He was attached to the army medical corps and taken prisoner by the Germans in 1940. Released from camp somewhat earlier than the other prisoners, supposedly on grounds of ill health, he returned to the capital. He resigned his teaching position in 1944, after the liberation of his country by the Allies. By that time his name as a dramatist, philosopher and novelist was well established.

PUBLIC LIFE

The bitter lesson of defeat in the war had demonstrated to Sartre the value of solidarity and the necessity to commit oneself and stand by to defend one's ideals with arms if need be. After the liberation he plunged into public activity. He experimented with founding a political party, the Rassemblement Démocratique Révolutionnaire, and started publishing a political-ideological journal, *Les temps modernes* (*Modern Times*). He took extended trips abroad, notably to Canada, the United States (1945), the Soviet Union and Cuba, contributing articles about his experiences to the major Paris dailies. He wrote a study on anti-Semitism, staunchly supported the independence of Algeria and condemned atrocities against the Arabs, came out against racial discrimination in the American South, and generally supported movements and groups whose objectives he considered praiseworthy, usually from the point of view of the defense and support of the underprivileged, oppressed or ostracized, as he saw them. In 1964 he turned down the Nobel Prize for Literature, a gesture of defiance against official honors that he says he does not covet.

ADULT PRIVATE LIFE

As a teacher, Sartre earned the affection of his students, many of whom regretted his resignation in 1944. His biographers generally agree that he is a loyal and generous friend, though he involved himself in public controversy with Albert Camus, one of his long-time associates, over political matters. An unresolved point in this connection is his participation in a resistance group during the occupation years. His enemies allege that Sartre left the organization when the danger of arrest grew substantial. Though out of contempt for social **conventions** Sartre has never married, he lived for many years with Simone de Beauvoir, the novelist and journalist. He is said to have recently adopted a daughter. Since his rise to fame, Sartre has financially helped scores of individuals in need and has shown himself supremely indifferent to matters of money.

EARLY FICTION

His first writings reveal the author as an anarchist, a man condemning society for what it is, yet convinced of the ultimate futility of existence. The narrator of "Érostratus," Pierre in "The Room" and to some extent even the **protagonist** of Nausea are

5

rebels, but their revolt exhausts itself in some abortive act or useless gesture. Pablo in "The Wall" is ready to sacrifice himself for his convictions, only to discover that these convictions become emptied of significance in the shadow of death. The short stories and *Nausea* are probing psychological studies of a disenchanted, skeptical generation by one of its members. As far as the style is concerned, his first novel already shows Sartre possessing an accent of his own, though it is not unrelated to the context of French literary movements of the period. The style of *Nausea* is clipped, trenchant, witty, striving for no effects of harmony, balance and serene beauty such as cultivated by writers of earlier generations. This new toughness, as one might term it, had had its precursors; it can already be found in the youthful arrogance of Rimbaud; Sartre must have learned a great deal from Céline too, whose L'Église (The Church) provided the motto for *Nausea*. This style deceptively resembles common speech, but upon closer examination turns out to be contrived. The short stories were published a year after *Nausea*, but most of them actually predate the novel. Their style is not uniform, though they do not by any means suggest the pen of a beginner. Critical opinion has considered "The Childhood of a Leader" the highest achievement in the volume; it has been called the greatest short story written since the turn of the century. This piece is truly remarkable for its psychological penetration, its daring sincerity and the incantatory quality with which it recreates the atmosphere of childhood. Its tone is different from most of Sartre's other writing and suggests the influence of Flaubert, the undisputed master of restrained French prose.

DRAMA

Sartre's specific contribution as a playwright lies in his extraordinary ability to show that metaphysics is more interesting, indeed exciting, than cloak-and-dagger mysteries or portrayals of sexual depravity. All the plays belong to his second stage, that is, they present a more positive, less destructive picture than his prewar production. *The Flies*, first produced in 1943, was not well received, but, a year later, *No Exit*, by virtue of its simplicity and easy intellectual accessibility, enjoyed wide popular success. The Orestes of *The Flies* is an authentic hero, the first one Sartre ever created. Perhaps he had to go back over two thousand years in history to find one, for in the concrete circumstances of contemporary society it would have been difficult to picture one without traces of bad faith. Goetz, central character in the *Devil and the Good Lord*, realizes that anarchistic rebellion is no solution; one must join an organized revolutionary movement in order to serve humanity. But his last play, The Prisoner of Altona, reverts to a former attitude of pessimism, even though the older Sartre, seeing things in their complexity, injects elements of greatness and human tragedy even into the forbidding father figure, previously an exclusive object of loathing for him.

Notwithstanding the fact that Sartre is uncannily skillful in illustrating his main philosophical themes-man's freedom, the liquid quality of consciousness, our desire to possess others, the importance of our image as reflected in the consciousness of other people-like most modern playwrights he nevertheless resorts to melodramatic solutions and other non-intrinsic, surprise-producing effects from time to time. One of these can be schematically described as the situation in which A does not know that B realized all the time exactly what A was hoping to hide from him. Much of *Dirty Hands* is built on this schema. Another variation is to have a character make a revealing statement about himself only to make us realize five minutes later that he said it to hide something lying even deeper which, in turn, was a mere mask to veil a more underlying truth, etc., until the spectator feels that he is being led on a wild-goose chase that helps the author to create dramatic tension but does not elucidate anything about the person pictured. Sartre uses some of the old theatrical stocks-in-trade, such as soldiers, townsfolk and old women, to lighten the tragic tone or produce stage effects, in ways that one would deem inconsistent with his theory of personality. They nevertheless contribute to what we call "good theater" in the sense of audience acceptance and entertainment.

POSTWAR NOVELS

They consist of *The Roads to Freedom*, originally projected as a four-part cycle. Only three volumes have been published and indications are that the fourth one will never be completed. In them he further modified his technique. His new belief in the importance of responsibility, in the interrelated nature of human actions, prompted him to adopt the method used by Dos Passos in U.S.A. and Manhattan Transfer: without continuity he shows how certain people, scattered all over Europe, react to the world situation in the months immediately preceding the war. Though he again uses the medium to illustrate his favorite philosophical and political themes, it would be a mistake to label these novels as mere romans a theme: the characters described are usually convincing, not mere paper figures with ideas hung upon them. They also show Sartre's growing concern with participation, his thirst for life as expressed in dynamic action and the ambivalent attraction that people who are aggressive and bold enough to assert themselves possess for him. He loathes them because they are crude and irresponsible and, we are tempted to say, because he envies them; on the other hand, at times he cannot hide his admiration because they represent an aim that he would wish to achieve.

Though philosophically he has often demonstrated that man's search for being must lead to failure, he entertains the idea that when we completely dissolve ourselves in action we can taste supreme moments. Mathieu, the central figure in the cycle, transubstantiates himself in this fashion toward the end of his life and, even though his annihilation is near, he is more truly alive at the moment of death than he has ever been during his frustrated lifetime. Another phenomenon worth pointing out is the author's predisposition in these volumes to attribute unenviable physical traits to his social and political enemies. When we read about someone with a severe case of halitosis or enviable physical traits to his social and political enemies. When larly vicious example of moral depravity from the Sartrean point of view. This is not worthy of a writer having Sartre's intellectual stature and perspective.

THEORETICAL WORKS

Throughout the ages, many philosophers, theologians and novelists have noted that there was something singularly unsatisfactory and frustrating about the human condition. They have attributed this to divine punishment, the consequences of original sin, the coexistence of an immaterial soul and a mortal body or the limitless nature of our ideas as contrasted with the finitude of what we can accomplish. Around the turn of the century a new direction in philosophy propounded that the world was fundamentally irrational, that is, it could not be comprehended with our logic. A group of modern novelists and playwrights follow along essentially similar lines when they describe the universe as an absurd one. Many contemporary writers feel that in the past the dominant tendency has been to portray life as it should or might be as against what it really is. They do not believe that the realists or the naturalists have gone far enough. Although they depicted misery and degradation, they showed human reality in a static, anatomical manner.

Man, these recent writers argue, is not an easily definable, petrified creature: he is full of contradictions, he rarely tells the truth about himself, and literature in the past contented itself with describing him in conventional, stereotyped, schematic ways that most of us like to accept but that do not reflect him as he actually is. These new authors cultivate sincerity as the highest literary objective. Sartre's central initial human experience as well as his main **metaphysical** aid literary contribution, has been to realize and demonstrate not only that people are hypocritical and mendacious but that it is impossible for them to be sincere. The gift of the 700-odd pages of *Being and Nothingness* is that man is not what he is and therefore he could not be truthful about himself even if he wished to. In this lies the tragedy of the human condition according to Sartre. As an expression of this conviction his thought is unique and revolutionary.

Sartre's theoretical writing and fiction are closely linked with each other. The novels, short stories and plays are readable in themselves, but they are dependent for their significance on the philosophy. This does not, however, mean that all of Sartre's fiction consistently interprets his ideas. Nor does it imply, of course, that the ideas represented are always sound. Sartre can argue with disarming logic, but we must bear in mind that in the final analysis he is not a rationalist. This puts him in a peculiar position, for he aspires to demonstrate with reason that which is irrational. In fact, it is not difficult to show how his theory is riddled with contradictions. As a system, Sartrean existentialism does not hold water. Sartre's excellence lies neither in his system nor in his method, the latter having been borrowed from the German phenomenologists, but in the revealing nature of his insights.

CRITICISM

Sartre must be recognized as one of the most original and incisive critics of our time. In this **genre** his literary talent and dialectic form a happy union. The verbal pyrotechnics seem to be less out of place here than in his philosophy. Several of the essays included in the three volumes of *Situations* are true masterpieces; Sartre's treatment is usually the most probing and modern interpretation ever published on the respective author. He often relies heavily on biographical data but he also excels in stylistic analysis. Two of his critical pieces, *Baudelaire* and *On Genet*, are separate volumes. The latter, notwithstanding its virtues, shows Sartre's technique at its worst. Its reasoning is labyrinthine, and when one divests it of the striking phraseology, the brilliance of the **imagery** and the suppleness of the **syntax**, it frequently turns out to be disappointingly shallow and even repetitious. Sartre's contention that Genet writes "pour épater les bourgeois" (to shock the middle class) and that his works were purposely devised so as not to make sense, in order to trap the reader, is much more pertinent to Sartre himself than Genet. It is Sartre's own product that resembles a monumental hide-and-seek, and he rather than Genet is the one who has created an intricate maze without a blueprint.

A DOUBLE MORALITY

Sartre has long held out the prospect of writing a new ethic but as of this date its publication appears to be more distant than ever. Existentialism is a moral philosophy, yet the public have had to shift for themselves as best they could trying to discover its implications. *Existentialism* contains a very crude outline of an ethic; *On Genet* comes closest to presenting a theory on right and wrong conduct. But what we can gather from these works is unsatisfactory. In many respects they suggest as their author a precocious high-school student who wants to impress his schoolmates with cynical statements in which he, however, does not believe. First, Sartre is fond of the idea that there is no true subjective evil, as we always do everything for some good we hope to obtain. What, then, is that which we call evil in our everyday language? It is, he claims, simply the projection of that part of ourselves which we do not acknowledge. While Sartre maintains that there exists no real evil, he calls certain types of conduct mistaken ones. All these "mistakes" of moral judgment are predicated by him on the individual's failure to act according to his freedom. But as Sartre holds that we all inwardly know that we are free, mistaken conduct simply boils down to bad faith, that is, lying to ourselves.

In other words, Sartre's evil-for is there any other than a verbal difference between "faulty" or "wrong" conduct? - is insincerity. But his metaphysics predicates insincerity as the foundation of the human condition! It is easy to see why Sartre would have great difficulty in formulating an existentialist ethics. To be sure, Sartre's fiction is abundant in cases where characters are guilty of "faulty" moral standards in the sense that they mask their freedom from themselves, accepting some kind of ready-made image of their personality. Yet all of his works implicitly affirm the existence of a moral order over and above his acknowledged principles. This second, implied code condemns brutality, cruelty and aggressiveness; it rejects the institution of the scapegoat; it censures the maltreatment of the weak by the powerful; it reproves the suppression of the poor, the ostracizing of any segment of society on the basis of racial or other prejudice. In Sartrean theory there is only one notion: that of responsibility, in the defense of these implied values. but responsibility seems to be a later, extraneous addition to the doctrine developed by the French philosopher, and it only slightly lessens the paradox of a double morality in his works.

AN INTENSELY HUMAN WORLD

The considerations we have offered above do not exhaust Sartre's appeal as an author. What differentiates him from others is an approach and an emotional pitch: Sartre has been influenced by many philosophers, such as Descartes, Schopenhauer, Nietzsche, Bergson, Husserl and Heidegger, and writers, such as Dostoevsky, Pirandello, Gide, Céline, Dos Passos and Hemingway. Yet his production is no mere aggregate of the ideas and techniques of these men. When we read Sartre we are struck by another quality: the intensity of his preoccupation with human problems. The eyes of the keen, hypersensitive observer who wants to get at the very roots, who wants to seize the stuff of life and transcribe it at its inception, are already apparent in his first published work. Sartre's world is exclusively, almost suffocatingly human; he has no interest in nature, animals or the beauty of landscapes and scenery. His undivided and passionate attention is focused on mankind. While reading him, the atmosphere we are transported in seems thicker, the scene is highly illuminated; nothing can escape us that is of any importance. We see through the mental eyes of one who perceives and feels with agonizing acuteness. This experience alone is an adequate reward for the reader.

CRITICAL REACTION

Sartre first gained acceptance as an author through a number of technical publications on philosophical subjects: *Psychology and Imagination, The Transcendence of the Ego, The Emotions*, etc. These only earned him short notices in professional journals. After his name had suddenly become notorious during the last years of the war, philosophers saw an upstart in him, an intruder into the domain of their serene discipline, and usually judged his theoretical work severely, declaring either that its conceptual content was negligible, being a mere repetition of what others had said before him, or that his brand of existentialism was not a philosophy at all. Martin Heidegger, at present the greatest name in German existentialism, stated in an interview in 1950 that he had read *Being and Nothingness* and believed that Sartre was a good writer, but not a philosopher. Catholic thinkers (H. de Lubac, Gabriel Marcel) tended to disagree with him, but interestingly they were among the first who gave his ideas a hearing. This is because Sartre, though an atheist tackles questions in a manner that is familiar to scholasticism: the distinction between essence and existence was one of the keystones in the thinking of Church scholars during the Middle Ages. Academic British and American philosophical circles on the whole either disregarded him or reacted coolly to his theories, for most of them hold that metaphysics, in which Sartre's chief contribution lies, is a largely discredited and outmoded branch of philosophy. Finally, both Marxist and non-Marxist determinists have rejected Sartre's doctrine on freedom. His irrationalism has likewise been condemned in both East and West by philosophers who believe in the ability of the human mind to comprehend reality (cf. G. Lukacs, *The Destruction of Reason*). Sartrean philosophy has made few converts, yet its impact has been considerable. Though most professional philosophers discount it as a consistent **exposition** of any doctrine or as a genuine application of any method, including phenomenology, the brilliance and accuracy of some of its observations and theories have impressed a growing number of them (Desan, Campbell, Nathanson, Hook) during recent years.

Literary critics have not been unanimously enthusiastic about Sartre's writings either. While *Nausea* was greeted in France as an interesting experiment even by conservative critics like Edmond Jaloux, the London Times Literary Supplement merely described it as "pretentious." His first play, *The Flies*, got poor notices in the papers at the time. However, a few years later *Dirty Hands* met with considerable critical acclaim. The cycle *The Roads to Freedom* was declared a failure by several critics (Philip Thody, R. M. Albérès) because it remains unfinished. Others (Henri Peyre, Hazel Barnes) saw it more positively, but the consensus tends to favor *Nausea* over *Roads to Freedom* as Sartre's best novel. Ever since the mid-fifties the leading literary journals, while far from rendering him unanimous praise, have been forced to regard him as one of the most important writers of our time: they can no longer dismiss Sartre with a shrug. His public reputation has steadily grown, too. Most of his later plays had long runs in Paris and they, as well as his other fiction, have become best sellers all over the world, including the United States. On the other hand, the younger writers no longer regard him as an object of imitation or adulation. Literature moves on, and a new generation feels it their right and duty to dethrone their elders. But Sartre has already inscribed his name on the annals of literary history and his fame will in all likelihood outlive his youngest critics.

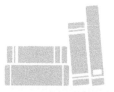

NAUSEA

INTRODUCTION

Published in 1938, *Nausea* was Sartre's first novel. He had previously published only one short story, L'ange du morbide (*The Morbid Angel,* untranslated). To the surprise of his editors, it was an immediate success. Though for the public his name conveyed notoriety rather than fame, he established himself as a young avant-garde writer whose development was to be watched. *Nausea* is a **metaphysical** diary supposedly kept by a certain Antoine Roquentin, a historian at work on a monograph dealing with the Marquis de Rollebon, eighteenth-century profligate and diplomatist. The fictional framework is that the journal has been found among Roquentin's papers and is being now published posthumously. At the time of the writing (1932), Roquentin was thirty years old and had already lived at Bouville, the Marquis's birthplace, for close to three years. The diary consists of consecutive entries titled, "Tuesday," "nine p.m.," "two hours later," etc., and is composed in the first person singular.

PLOT STRUCTURE

The first entry is prompted by a disquieting experience that Roquentin cannot explain to himself. He is at the harbor of

Bouville, watching some youngsters ricocheting pebbles over the water. He picks up a pebble and is suddenly overcome by a sense of disgust. A few days later he dismisses this sensation as ridiculous. But in the next entry he notes that something must have happened in his life during the past few weeks, even though he cannot say what. He is fearful of what seems to be going on, either in himself or in the external world. He would like to talk about it to someone; however, he knows only two persons in town. For the first time in his life, loneliness weighs on him. Objects are beginning to annoy him. He is afraid of touching them, as if they were living creatures. Now he thinks that the other day it was the touch of the pebble that caused his malaise. It was a kind of sweetish disgust, a feeling of nausea in his hand.

He is almost beginning to doubt the historical reality of the Marquis de Rollebon. None of the facts can be proved. Everything about him is hypothetical. He appears to be more imaginary than a fictitious character. Roquentin is given to contemplating his own image in the mirror these days. He comprehends nothing about it. Other people's faces have expressions. But in the mirror he only sees eyes, ears, a nose, a mouth: senseless details. He wonders if other men have so much difficulty in judging their own faces. Perhaps it is impossible to understand one's own face. Or is it because he is alone? He goes to his cafe. He looks at the people and the walts and he is again overcome by nausea. He asks the waitress to put on his favorite record, an old ragtime tune, with the **refrain**, "Some of these days you'll miss me honey." Suddenly the nausea disappears. He feels his body become hard and solid. He is happy. Then he goes to the movies.

On Thursday Roquentin visits the municipal library. He finds his acquaintance, Ogier P., a white-collar worker whom he has nicknamed the Self-Taught Man, already installed there. As he muses over the seemingly unconnected nature of the Self-Taught Man's readings, he is struck by the fact that the authors' names have been Lambert, Langlois, Larbaletrier, Lastex, etc. They follow in alphabetical order. He discovers that the Self-Taught Man is engaged in a project to read the entire contents of the library.

Roquentin writes that he can see the future. He looks out on the street and watches an old woman pass by. He knows where she will be ten minutes from now. He wonders whether he just sees or predicts her gestures. In the present he feels abandoned, rejected. He tries in vain to recapture the past; he cannot escape. The Self-Taught Man comes to see him at his hotel room. Roquentin has promised to show him some pictures from his travels (he had traveled extensively in Central Europe, North Africa and the Far East). The Self-Taught Man hangs on Roquentin's words as the latter lets fall a few cursory remarks about the lands he has traveled in. The Self-Taught Man asks him if he had many adventures. After finishing his present project at the library, which will take him another six years, the Self-Taught Man hopes to go on a voyage to the Near East with a group of teachers and students that go there annually.

As the little man leaves, Roquentin questions himself whether he did really have any adventures. Until now he used to tell himself that, though his present life had no great brilliance, he had had some exquisite moments in London, Meknes, or Tokyo. Now he realizes that all this time he has been lying to himself. Adventures are only in books. The next day he reflects on this some more. The question is: why is it impossible to have adventures? The most banal of events become adventures as soon as one relates them. This is what misleads people. One day, in Hamburg, Roquentin was sitting in a cafe with Erna, a girl he had little interest in. While Erna went to the rest room, he started to tell himself what had happened since his arrival in Germany. It seemed to him that Erna was part of an adventure. But when she came back he despised the girl. Now he understands that the reason for his repulsion was that he had to start living again and that the impression of adventure had fled him. His aim was to arrange his life in such a way as to resemble the story of a life as one recalls it. This, he now discovers, was an utter impossibility.

Comment

Roquentin's experiences parallel and illustrate certain aspects of Sartre's philosophy as expounded in *Being and Nothingness*. Sartre wrote *Nausea* while he was already at work on the first draft of his great opus on metaphysics. When he describes the old woman on the street, he exemplifies his conception that man is a project. Sartre took this from the phenomenologists who term the process whereby man projects himself into the future "transcendence." Escaping into the past is one of the modes in which man tries to forget about his contingency. Like the other human ex-stasis (flights from the present), it must end in failure: one cannot recapture the past. Its charm is in the fact that it is an in-itself (en-soi), i.e., it exists by itself, it is definite, unchangeable, and lacks the anguish that characterizes the present with its continuous hesitations between choices to be made. Roquentin reflectively discovers that his past, while it was still the present, did not contain any of the beauty that he now ascribes to it precisely because it has become part of past experience.

The next day is Sunday, the day of the week that Roquentin abhors the most. He walks down Tournebride Street, which is in the section of the town that the bourgeois have recently taken over from the lower classes. The burghers are out, parading in their provincial finery, going to and coming from Mass. In the afternoon the people become somewhat depressed: the specter of Monday has already appeared on the horizon. But Roquentin is overcome by a sudden feeling of bliss: he knows that he is himself and there; he is involved in the moment; he thinks that something is going to happen, he breathes a scent of adventure in the air; then his enthusiasm suddenly deflates. Behind him a ghastly social event is taking place: the agonizing death of a Sunday afternoon.

Comment

Roquentin's elation is due to an intuitive grasp of the passage of time as the first lights go on. The people of Bouville will pass away just as their precious Sunday has come to ashes.

On Tuesday, Roquentin receives a letter in the mail. It is from Anny, an English girl Roquentin used to love. She is going to be passing through Paris next month, and asks Roquentin to come there to see her. Roquentin believes he still loves this unconventional, volatile, impulsive young woman whose ambition was to achieve "perfect moments." He is looking forward to their meeting after six years of separation. On Saturday Roquentin goes on one of his periodic visits to the Bouville Museum. The portraits of one hundred fifty eminent Bouvillians look down on him from the walls: the elite of the town between 1875 and 1910, painted with scrupulous **realism**. Shipowners, industrialists, businessmen: the mainstays of law and order, representatives of the upper-middle class, backbone of French society during the Third Republic. He pauses for a moment in front of the portrait of Pacome, the merchant, and he understands what separates him from most of these people. Roquentin's thoughts cannot touch Pacome, but he judges

Roquentin with implacable calm. He questions even Roquentin's very right to exist. Roquentin feels that he exists like a microbe, a plant compared to these men. Everything always rightfully belonged to them: they did their duty, never questioning themselves. They were true leaders.

Comment

Roquentin, the rootless intellectual, a man without allegiances, whether to party, family, nation, or humanity, loathes both the self-confident power and hypocrisy of the French upper classes that the canvasses on the wall symbolize to him. Roquentin is free, he knows himself, he is aware of the nothingness Sartre claims yawns inside us. The men whose paintings are on the wall never exercised introspection, they acted as if they were machines. They were in bad faith, salauds like most leaders. They were committed, but they did not feel their responsibility and hid behind the facade of middle-class respectability in their dealings with each other and with the lower classes. The basic difference between them and Roquentin is that they behaved as though they were necessary, while the latter knows that he is contingent, expendable and unwanted.

Roquentin stands in the center of the hall, realizing that he is neither a respectable grandfather, nor a father, nor even a husband. He wonders if he is not a mere appearance. Another member of the gallery is Doctor Parrottin. He smiles affably, with an expression of forgiveness. He was a leader of youth, a confidential counselor, a trusted friend. His secret was that he understood everyone. He extended his forgiving smile to his rebellious students, teaching them little by little their responsibilities, their duties as members of France's elite. Roquentin leaves the museum with a sense of contempt.

Next Monday he knows that he cannot go on with the Rollebon monograph. He is sitting with a blank sheet in front of him, staring at it. The true nature of the present becomes clear to him. The present is what exists, and whatever is not present does not exist-not at all, not even in one's thoughts. Now he discovers that things are entirely as they appear, there is nothing behind them. He is immensely discouraged. Rollebon has died for a second time. Roquentin has realized that the past does not exist, and that is the end of the Marquiz de Rollebon.

Comment

Roquentin's revelation about the nature of things is the point of departure of phenomenology, the new direction in German philosophy that Sartre studied under the guidance of its chief exponent, Edmund Husserl, in Berlin in the winter of 1933-1934. His distress is caused by his being forced to admit that the Marquis served for him merely as a distraction, in the sense of an evasion, all this time. He had been trying to live through Rollebon. Or rather, Rollebon had been robbing him of his vitality. Now Roquentin is totally free: more precisely, he has recognized his total freedom.

He keeps repeating to himself, "I exist." The body lives alone, by itself, once it has started. But thought is continued by the ego. The process of thinking is what one calls oneself. I exist because I think. Roquentin leaves his hotel, buys a paper, glances at the headline. The body of the raped girl, Lucienne, has been found. Her body still exists. She no longer does. He watches a handsome mustachioed gentleman pass by, with the red ribbon of the Legion of Honor on his lapel. How wonderful it must feel to be nothing but a Legion of Honor and a moustache, he reflects. No one can see the rest. All these salauds have a right to exist. They have the right not to think.

Comment

Roquentin's considerations about the body do not seem to coincide with Sartre's as presented in *Being and Nothingness*. There is reason to conclude that the hypothesis according to which body and mind are one was formulated later by the author. If the body "lives alone," it is a separate entity from the mind. Such a theory leads to subjectivistic idealism, to either an unbridgeable gulf between thought and matter or the denial of the existence of matter. This was inherent in *Discours de la méthode*, Descartes' famous disquisition that has greatly influenced the course of later French philosophy. Sartre is a Cartesian inasmuch as he believes in the axiom, "cogito ergo sum" (I think, therefore I am), but in *Being and Nothingness* he tried to overcome the difficulties inherent in idealism. The linking together of body and mind in his subsequently published work represents one of his efforts in this direction.

On Wednesday Roquentin lunches with the Self-Taught Man, who listens to the historian's pronouncements with infinite respect, but notices the tone of sarcasm in Roquentin's words and is somewhat offended by it. He grasps the fact that to Roquentin existence is futile and tells him about a book entitled *Is Life Worth Living*, written by an American. The author believed in optimistic voluntarism. He concluded that life was indeed meaningful if one gave it sense. One should act first, involve oneself in life. Action itself will supply the meaning of one's commitment. But, the Self-Taught Man goes on, he does not need to search for meaning as far as that. There is a goal for him: it is called mankind. He is a humanist. To make his point clearer, the Self-Taught Man relates the story of his life. Before the war, (the First World War), he lived a solitary life without really knowing it. He was staying with his parents, but their relationship was not a happy one. Now it seems to him as though he had been dead during those years. When the war came, he volunteered and was taken prisoner by the Germans in 1917. He affirms that in the concentration camp he learned to have faith in mankind. When it was raining the Germans used to herd all the prisoners into an empty hangar. It was there one day that, pressed tight among hundreds of human beings, he understood for the first time that he loved people like brothers.

After the war he missed the communion with people that he enjoyed during his captivity. Again he was alone and he would have committed suicide had he not been struck by the fact that no one would have regretted his passing. In 1921 he joined the Socialist Party and he has been happy ever since. Now he is never alone. That is, he never has the sensation of loneliness, even though he does not know many people. Roquentin ponders the Self-Taught Man's words. He has known many humanists: radicals, rightists, leftists, Catholics. They all hated one another. Just as individuals, of course; as men, in the abstract, they professed to love each other. He tries to show the Self-Taught Man that he does not like people either but he does not insist, he feels sympathetic toward him; after all, his only fault is ignorance, his good will is genuine. He even feels remorseful about spoiling the Self-Taught Man's speech: the poor fellow must have been looking forward to this luncheon all week. He has few opportunities to talk.

Comment

The Self-Taught Man typifies what Sartre termed elsewhere the "spirit of earnestness" (l'esprit du sérieux). He speaks of Learning, Culture, Reading and the like with the seriousness of the hopelessly ignorant. He has no perspective. He thinks that education consists in reading the contents of a library from A to

Z, much in the fashion of the college undergraduate who takes Chinese Poetry one semester and Developmental Psychology the next, hoping that he will eventually be turned out a perfect "product." But an accumulation of facts is not knowledge. It is ironical that Sartre should have put into the mouth of this harmless but absurd creature some of the theories in which he was later to believe. The thesis of the book *Is Life Worth Living*, despite the naivete of the title, uncannily resembles the doctrine the French philosopher has since evolved himself. The prophetic **irony** of the Self-Taught Man's words is all the more striking as Sartre was to learn the value of commitment in the next war. Like the Self-Taught Man, he joined the French Army and was taken prisoner by the Germans. And in one of his first pronouncements after the liberation he professed to be a humanist! To be sure, he maintains that his humanism is of a different sort. But, beyond the shadow of a doubt, his ideas changed as well as his terminology.

The Self-Taught Man goes on with his panegyric to mankind and Roquentin feels like vomiting. Nausea has come again. He feels the dessert knife against his fingers. He lets it drop. Now the pieces of the jigsaw puzzle have all fallen in place: the touch of the pebble, with which it all started; other nauseas afterwards. From time to time, things start existing in one's hand. Suddenly Roquentin notices that the Self-Taught Man has shrunk back on his chair. Roquentin wonders whether his face looks frightening. Everyone in the restaurant is watching him. He hurriedly bids good-be to the Self-Taught Man and crosses the dining room in the midst of embarrassed silence. Yet in the last moment he cannot resist turning back, in order to let his features be engraved in their memory. They thought he was human, Roquentin reflects bitterly, and now they know he is outside the fold. Later that evening he further ponders over the relationship of things that have caused nausea in him. They have only one thing in common: they are unwanted, too much (de trop) to cope with. Just as he also is unnecessary. "Absurdity" is another term to cover what he is thinking of, he writes. He has found the secret of existence: everything goes back to the fact of a basic absurdity. To exist means simply to be there; the existent simply appear, they are undeductible. Everything is gratuitous, contingent.

Comment

This revelation of the ultimate nature of being is the **climax** of the novel. Nausea is the intuitive awareness of the contingency of all beings. By contingency Sartre means lack of necessity. Reality was not caused by anything and is not kept in existence for any reason. It is interesting to point out that in *Being and Nothingness* he refers to the concept of nausea as a perpetual awareness of the contingency of the body, an apprehension of oneself as existent. Nausea, he writes, is my taste. On the other hand, in the novel Roquentin speaks of the contingency of all the objects around him as well as his own contingency.

Roquentin decides that nothing can tie him to Bouville any longer. He leaves for Paris, as he intends to see Anny there. When he goes to her hotel his first impression is that she has put on weight. They talk about some of the things that have happened to them since they last saw each other; then the conversation drifts to Anny's favorite subject, "perfect moments." It is all finished, she says, no more perfect moments; they do not exist. In her childhood, her favorite book was Michelet's *History of France*. She had a beautiful edition, with colored plates. She used to look forward to seeing the scenes Michelet was describing, for the colored plates were never opposite the page where the scene was described. This is how she first conceived the idea of privileged situations, that is, rare, significant **episodes** in one's life. In each privileged situation, there are appropriate attitudes and gestures, while other actions and words are strictly forbidden. Now she has discovered that there are no perfect moments, because there are no privileged situations to begin with. She used to imagine that there was such a thing as love, or hatred. There is only oneself who loves or hates. And oneself is always the same thing. Roquentin realizes that her mental development has paralleled his own. With him, it is the illusion of adventures that has gone. He still loves Anny, though he feels little physical attraction now toward her aging body. Anny does not believe that if they lived together it would help either of them. She is going to leave for London the next evening, but she does not want him to see her off. She will be with a man who is now keeping her.

Despite Anny's wish, Roquentin goes to the railroad station the following day, but he remains in the background. Her companion was a tall, handsome man in a camel's-hair coat. He looked like an Egyptian. Just before the train started, Anny noticed Roquentin and kept looking at him with inexpressive eyes. Roquentin feels free, but his freedom resembles death. He has now learned that one can only lose in life; none but the salauds think that they can win. Now, he decides, he will do the same as Anny: he will survive himself.

He goes back to Bouville to settle his affairs. He witnesses an unpleasant scene in the municipal library. Two young high school boys who want to ridicule the Self-Taught Man sit down next to him and make advances to him. The Self-Taught Man is caught in the trap and is exposed and struck by the library attendant. Roquentin restrains the attendant, but it is already too late: the Self-Taught Man will never be able to go back to the library. He refuses Roquentin's offer to accompany him to the

27

corner pharmacy and they part at the stairs. Roquentin goes to his cafe, the Rendez-Vous des Cheminots. He says good-bye to Mme. Jeanne, who operates the establishment (she has appealed to him physically, but intellectually she means nothing to him). The waitress puts on his favorite ragtime melody for him. He listens to the girl singing. The voice does not exist; it is, it has nothing of the quality of other objects that reveal themselves as being too much. Roquentin is going to go back to live in Paris. As he is waiting for the train to arrive, he formulates one project in his mind: to write a novel about himself, so that people who will come later may nod with recognition when hearing his name, and think of a sandy-haired chap who used to sit about wasting his time in cafes.

CHARACTER ANALYSIS OF ANTOINE ROQUENTIN

The texture of his life closely approximates Sartre's own at the time. Sartre, too, was a bachelor living in nihilistic detachment. He taught philosophy at the lycée of Le Havre from 1934 to 1936, while doing research on his **metaphysical** disquisition. Le Havre, like Bouville, is a seaport, with proportions and layout resembling Bouville's. But, unlike the Sartre of the 1930s, Roquentin is a man of the world, well traveled and uninhibited. He is tall and physically powerful. It has been suggested by one perceptive critic, Albérès, that Roquentin represents an ennobled version of the author: Sartre as he would have liked to see himself. We should bear in mind that Roquentin's aloofness from social participation was regarded as an ideal by many French intellectuals, and the tradition of the poet as a person of high sensitivity, living outside society, has been almost a literary commonplace in France ever since the romantic period. Roquentin is an outsider, but not an outcast: he has severed his ties because he scorns people, whom he finds for the most part too unintelligent, bigoted and mean to bother with. His sympathies are few; he pities the Self-Taught Man and occasionally has glimpses of compassion for people whom he feels to be victims of the social machinery. Yet it would be going too far to affirm that he is the Sartrean hero-not even of the corresponding period in the author's spiritual evolution.

CRITICAL COMMENTARY ON NAUSEA

Bouville (from boue = mud, mire): Mudtown, France. Sartre's repugnance to provincial standards and conventional and outmoded ways was elevated to the **metaphysical** plane in the present novel. With all due respect to Sartre as a philosopher, it is highly unlikely that this book would have ever been written but for the social context in which Sartre was moving. Yet, despite the protest against a narrow, uncomprehending milieu that is evident on every page from this angry young man of the thirties, he prefers to attribute his troubles to an ontological condition.

Not that an ontological interpretation is entirely unwarranted. Sartre holds that when man is thrown back on himself, that is, when he is alone, as Roquentin was, he obtains a clearer picture of his reality, his nothingness. The awareness of his basic emotional condition is then "projected" into the external world (this is not his terminology, but the concept is easier to grasp as projection). Nausea is associated with objects in the external world, too, since sense perceptions make up part of our consciousness. Now, Sartre contends that viscosity (la viscosité) is the most repulsive of states that physical phenomena can assume. Viscous things (le visqueux) absorb man as a for-itself as a blotter absorbs ink. Let us now recall the meaning of Bouville and the first encounter with nausea after picking up a pebble on the beach that was probably wet and muddy. The contingency of things first strikes Roquentin as he comes into contact with being in its most horrible form. The disquieting contingency of existing things is opposed to the singer's voice on the record, which signifies to Sartre the healing power of music that shows being to us as it should be. The voice, he states, does not merely exist, it is: great art transports us into another sphere that at least momentarily liberates us from contingency. We must again emphasize that these views reflect the young Sartre and do not necessarily coincide with his later doctrine.

THE WALL

(The story is a first person narrative, told by Pablo Ibbieta.) Pablo was interrogated together with two other Republicans (the faction opposing Franco in the Spanish Civil War of 1936-38), an Irishman by the name of Thomas Steinbock and an adolescent, Juan Mirbal. Pablo was accused of hiding a revolutionary leader in his home, Tom was a member of the International Brigade (a group of foreign volunteers), while Juan's only crime was that his brother was a prominent anti-Fascist. They led them to an unheated cell in the basement of the hospital building that was used by Franco's troops as a prison and soon let them know that they had been sentenced to death and would be shot next morning. A Belgian doctor came in with two guards to assist them. Pablo looked at the horror-stricken faces of the two other prisoners and understood that he too looked ghastly. He also noticed that he was perspiring copiously, though it was bitterly cold in the basement. He deeply resented the hypocritical solicitude of the Belgian who was studying their behavior from a scientific point of view. Tom told Pablo that he was already feeling the bullet wounds. But he could not understand his own death. He could visualize himself as a corpse, but even then it was still he who was looking at the corpse; what he could not perceive of was that life on earth would go on without him.

Pablo was the toughest of the three; he had a certain contempt for Tom's loquacity. He thought of his past life, of women, of his participation in the anarchist movement and now it seemed to him that the whole thing had been a lie. His life no longer had any value and he did not regret anything about it. He did not even wish to send a note to Concha, his mistress. The idea of his death appeared to be imprinted on all the objects around him: they had become more distant. Now he knew that even if someone came to tell him that he could go home unharmed nothing would have changed, for during these hours he had learned definitively that life could not last forever. Before, he used to act as if he had been immortal; from now on, he would live in the shadow of death: whether he had a day or a few years to live made no basic difference.

Comment

This passage clearly demonstrates that Sartre is too good a writer to abide by his doctrines. As a philosopher, he does not believe in death (see section on *Being and Nothingness*) as far as the subject is concerned, yet here he brilliantly shows the enormous tension that approaching death exerts on the individual.

Pablo was seeing and hearing through his body, but his body was no longer himself; he had the impression that he was tied to an enormous vermin. In the early morning hours Juan broke down completely. Finally the door opened and they took Tom and Juan away to be executed but left Pablo in the cell. An hour later he was interrogated again. They hoped to learn from him the whereabouts of Juan Gris. Pablo thought he knew where Gris was hiding: at his cousins', a few miles from town. But he made up his mind not to talk. At this time he was only wondering about one thing: the reasons for his own conduct. Since the revelation of the inevitability of death that morning, he no longer cared what would happen to Gris, or to the entire anarchist movement, for that matter. He found the whole scene absurd, the mustachioed interrogator ridiculous. In order to mislead them, Pablo said that Gris was hiding out in the cemetery, in one of the vaults or in the gravediggers' barracks. They immediately sent out a detachment and left Pablo alone. Half an hour later, the fat officer with the moustache came back and ordered Pablo to be taken back to jail, but this time not to solitary confinement. Pablo did not understand what had happened. He learned the truth later in the day from another man who had just been arrested. Gris had left his cousins' house and was hiding out in the cemetery when he was found by a detachment of soldiers and shot to death on the spot. When Pablo heard this he broke out in uncontrollable laughter.

Comment

It has been suggested, (notably in Claude Magny's *Les sandales d'Empédocle*), that the surprise ending was meant by the author as an expression of life's utter absurdity. However, it rather strikes us as a melodramatic solution. A coincidence such as this one would be unlikely to occur in real life, and if it did it would not prove the world's absurdity, it would simply be a tragic concurrence of events. The main purpose of the story is freedom: nothing can induce Pablo to reveal Juan Gris's whereabouts (that he involuntarily does is incidental). The story is closest to Sartre's postwar ideology, in that it may be interpreted to posit involvement as an ideal. Yet clearly the life of the individual is the ultimate value: when Pablo understands that he must die, his past actions lose all sense to him. In *No Exit, The Flies, Dirty Hands* and *Roads to Freedom* we manifestly have a different scale of values. "The Wall" represents a transition from another point of view, too. It is the most tautly written of Sartre's short stories, already suggesting the influence of contemporary American authors, mainly Dos Passos and Hemingway.

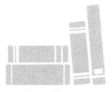

THE CHILDHOOD OF A LEADER

Everyone said Lucien looked charming in his angel's costume. Just like a little girl. Lucien was beginning to fear that the grown-ups would decide that he was actually a girl. He started to cry. He felt a little more secure in the car between Mommy and Daddy on the way home. They let him spend the night in the master bedroom. Next morning Lucien knew that something had happened during the night, but he did not wish to remember what. His mother was beside him, yet things were no longer the same; he saw her in a different light and dreaded her touch. He decided that he would avoid sleeping in his parents' room in the future.

Comment

Lucien has been jolted out of his childhood world by discovering that a certain intimacy existed between his mother and father that he had not suspected. Sartre believes that the infant or small child does not make a clear distinction between himself and his mother. The person first realizes his "otherness" when he is forced to acknowledge that his mother leads a life independent of him, that he is not the center of her existence. Now Lucien has started his search for identity.

Lucien wondered whether Mme. Fleurier was really his mother. He surmised that she was playing a role. At any rate, he stopped telling her that he would marry her when he grew up. Perhaps that certain night thieves stole his true Mommy and Daddy and replaced them. He got into the habit of imagining that he was an orphan. But more and more it seemed to the little boy that he was playing even when he was Lucien. He would have preferred to be like M. Bouffardier, who was ugly and serious. Nothing that happened to Lucien was in earnest. He rather liked grownups, especially the ones who were gloomy and wore a lot of clothes, so that one would not suppose them to do the sort of things little boys do. Lucien knew that children should love their mothers and once when he was alone he kept repeating to himself, "I love Mommy." On that day he realized that he did not love her. Yet he behaved so much more considerately toward her. In order to find out what was inside, Lucien broke all his toys. He was disappointed: things were not for real either. War broke out and M. Fleurier was drafted but soon came back to take charge of his factory again. Lucien fell into a kind of torpor. He would often pick his nose or smell his fingers; he became sullen. Grownups paid less attention to him since his golden locks had been cut off.

Comment

It may be worth noting that, in the first volume of his autobiography, *The Words* (*Les Mots*), Sartre wrote that his mother lost interest in him when, upon having his hair cut short for the first time, she discovered that her son was not handsome.

In order to liven things up a bit, Lucien confided to his cousin, Riri, that he was a sleepwalker. This was not a simple lie. He thought that perhaps he had an alter ego, the real Lucien, who loved his parents and did not merely play at being Lucien. His real self, he imagined, lived at night. After he explained all about it to Riri, he felt a bit scared, for now he truly believed he was a sleepwalker.

Comment

This amusing little incident shows the power that words have over human beings. Once he had communicated his fancy, it assumed a kind of reality to the boy.

There was someone who knew about everything. His name was the Good Lord. Lucien despised Him, for He knew that Lucien did not love his parents, that he pretended to be a good little boy, that he did things with his hands he was not supposed to. To counteract this impression in the Lord's mind, from time to time Lucien would tell himself that he loved his darling, darling Mommy dearly.

But there would always remain a particle of doubt in his own heart about the truth of this statement; and God, what with His inquisitiveness, would look at just that particle. On Sundays, M. Fleurier would take his son by the arm and they would meet Daddy's workers. Lucien liked these men because they called him "sir." One day, returning from one of these walks, M. Fleurier explained to him what a leader was. Lucien listened attentively and asked his Daddy whether he too would become a leader. M. Fleurier nodded and said that he had Lucien brought into the world for that very purpose. Lucien was profoundly impressed.

Comment

According to Sartre, most people can be explained by an original choice or series of choices they made early in life. The decision to be a leader has given a definitive direction to Lucien's development: it has provided him with a scale of values, with something set and determined to be striven for.

In 1919 Mme. Fleurier enrolled her son at St. Joseph's Preparatory School. When she came to inquire how her son was doing, Father Gerromet explained to her that Lucien was a good worker, but very indifferent. Lucien was disturbed by this judgment and asked for permission to go to the boys' room. There he noticed that someone had scribbled on the wall a message to the effect that Lucien Fleurier was a beanpole. When he came back, he had to admit the correctness of this statement: he was taller than the other boys. He felt ill at ease. In the evening he looked at himself in the mirror. But he could not tell whether he was tall or small, he was just Lucien.

Comment

This is one of Lucien's first experiences of definitions that the outside world (notably, other than his parents) thrusts upon him. At home he cannot decide whether the accusation is deserved or not, for size is a comparative quality.

Mme. Fleurier was disconsolate that her graceful little boy was becoming such a gawky creature. Lucien reacted to this by sleeping through much of the day. When Lucien was about sixteen, the Fleuriers moved to Paris. There he was glad to see again his cousin, Riri. His cousin was poor in mathematics. Lucien helped him, but one day his mother told him that Riri, instead of being grateful, thought Lucien was conceited. Shaken by this latest accusation, Lucien passed through a new crisis. He was trying in vain to establish his identity and finally came to the conclusion that he did not exist. In the months that followed Lucien again tried to take refuge in somnolence. He also thought of writing a Treatise On Nothingness, considering the world to be a comedy without actors.

Comment

Lucien tries to find out what he is by simultaneous introspection. It is Sartre's contention that such a quest cannot yield any results. The argument against introspection is an old one and was made much of by Auguste Comte, the founder of positivism. As soon as one tries to observe what one's emotions and thoughts are, they disappear. To Sartre this is a proof that consciousness by itself is nothing: character cannot exist in the present. Notice the parallelism between Lucien's projected treatise and the title of Sartre's opus on metaphysics. The story should not be considered autobiographical, but the author projected many of his childhood experiences into Lucien.

On one of his walks Lucien met the son of Bouligaud, a worker at his father's factory. This was an important test of Lucien's leadership qualities. He gazed at the young man with self-confident pride, but he did not even seem to recognize Lucien. The encounter was a severe blow to young Fleurier. As a result, his conviction that the world did not exist grew considerably. He decided that a dissertation would not prove to people that they were nothing. A dramatic act was needed. Lucien would commit suicide, leaving behind a note saying that he killed himself because he did not exist. In turn, people would start wondering whether they existed. Lucien would be recognized as a great martyr.

Comment

It is ironical that the chief tenet of Sartrean ontology (i.e., consciousness is the introduction of nothingness into the world) is here presented as related to the psychological condition of a young boy who cannot find his place in society. It is particularly revealing that Lucien's belief is reinforced by his failure to assert himself as a leader. In other words, the author creates the impression that the idea that people do not exist was formulated by Lucien as a vengeance on a society that did not accept him as he wished to be accepted. His gesture is made to seem all the more absurd as the act of taking his own life implicitly proves that he does exist. On the other hand, when we ascribe a psychological motive to a statement, we do not thereby prove that the statement is incorrect. It only puts its author in a different light.

Lucien's morbid thoughts were interrupted by the beginning of a new school year. He was taking a pre-engineering curriculum. He became friends with Berliac, an eccentric young man interested in psychoanalysis. Berliac told Lucien that he desired his mother until he was fifteen. Lucien read Freud and his self-doubts were suddenly dissipated. He realized that he simply had a complex. He meditated about his complexes all day long. Yet after a time the complexes were getting on his nerves. For one thing, he could no longer look his mother in the eye.

One day, however, Lucien met an older friend of Berliac's, Bergère, a handsome man in his mid-thirties who was a surrealist. Lucien told him all about his anal-sadistic tendencies in choice Freudian terms. Bergère listened to him attentively and declared that Lucien's condition was one of confusion. Bergère proved to be a man of great understanding, but during a stay at a hotel over Easter vacation it became painfully evident that his absorbing interest in Lucien was not restricted to matters mental. Fearing that he might become a homosexual himself, Lucien never went to see Bergère again. He struck up a relationship with a woman, Maud, whom he was eventually to possess.

His spiritual development was influenced by Lemordant, a classmate of his, a man of few words and deliberate manners. Lemordant belonged to a movement of the extreme right. He told Lucien what his problem was: Lucien had been uprooted. Having been defined by so many other people, Lucien was at first wary of a new trap, but he found a sense of fraternity in Lemordant's group. Their feeling of togetherness was heightened by the murder of a middle-aged Jew who had been peacefully walking home when Lucien and his friends spotted him. Lucien was the one whose blow finally killed the little man. They were not caught in the adventure. Lucien gained in his reputation as a fierce anti-Semite. People respected his overpowering hatred for Jews. Once, when he was invited to a party, he would not shake the outstretched hand of a Jew and walked out furiously. The next day he was sorry about the incident and was thinking of excuses to make up when he met his friends and noticed the stature he had gained in their eyes through his act the previous night. This was a decisive experience for Lucien. He finally felt that he had found the real Lucien. He was to be found in the eyes of others, in the timid obedience of his friends and inferiors. He understood that this was the secret of being a leader. He felt himself pitiless and pure, like a blade of steel. He had rights to rely on; good solid objects like geometric forms. Now he was firmly convinced that his place under the sun had been determined before his birth, even before his father's marriage. He would drop Maud, he decided, and would marry a chaste provincial maiden who had been waiting for someone like him all her life. When the clock was striking noon, the person who got up from beside the cafe table was a new man, an adult, a leader among Frenchmen.

Lucien, defined in turn as a beanstalk, braggart, anal-sadist, deranged genius and uprooted provincial, has finally found the identification he was searching for. Were any of these identifications based on reality according to Sartre? There was a germ of truth in each: Lucien was tall, compared to others; Lucien was pleased by the fact that he understood mathematics better than his cousin; he was a sexual creature, similar to other males; he had original ideas that resulted from reflection; he had in some sense been deracinated when he moved to Paris. But all these definitions were directed at him as an in-itself, an object, a character, and thus missed the intimate reality of the human condition. Consciousness has no nature, it is fluid. "Character" has no relevance to human existence in the present.

Why was the label of anti-Semite a particularly attractive choice for Lucien? Essentially because it was totally arbitrary: he knew little about Jews, had no reason to like them or hate them as a race. People could not accuse him of personal motives. His new "convictions" gave him the opportunity to be feared and respected: they helped him toward the realization of his ultimate goal: leadership. By the end of the story he is totally in bad faith, he is a salaud par excellence, worshipping an image of himself, believing in his own birthright and God-given vocation to lead the French people.

THE FLIES

INTRODUCTION

Contemporary French dramatists have a predilection for borrowing themes from Greek mythology. Cocteau used the myth of Oedipus, Giraudoux the Trojan war, Anouilh the story of Antigone, to mention only a few examples. The temptation to do so is manifold: the playwright can take an archetypal human situation to try his hand at, the plot is there, he has an opportunity to show what new meaning he can infuse into it. He demonstrates that, though the accessories might change, man must face the same challenges in all ages. The historical setting lends itself to allegorical treatment: circumstances in ancient Greece may resemble those existing in our time; statements made by the characters have a ring of **irony**. It is particularly important to bear this in mind in connection with a man as involved in his society as Sartre professes to be; nothing could be farther from him than the cultivation of Greek tragedy for its own sake.

The Flies is a new Oresteia. The essentials of the myth are the following. Agamemnon, King of Argos, was killed by his wife, Clytemnestra, and her paramour, Aegisthus. Aegisthus subsequently married Clytemnestra and became the new king. Orestes, son of Agamemnon by Clytemnestra, was destined to be executed but was abandoned in the forest and brought up by kindly people. He returned to Argos as a young man, avenging his father's death by slaying both his mother and step-father. He was pursued by the Érinyes (Furies) for this act, until he reached Athens, where the Aeropagus acquitted him. Sartre made a few minor modifications on the plot in order to suit his purpose. It should be noted that he uses the Roman variant for the name of the supreme god, called Zeus by the Greeks. He perhaps did so because "Jupiter" sounds better on the stage or because it suggests Deus Pater (God the Father).

MAIN CHARACTERS

Orestes

Disinherited Prince of Argos, son of Agamemnon and Clytemnestra.

Tutor

A skeptic philosopher, responsible for Orestes' education.

Jupiter

Supreme god, disguised as an Athenian merchant.

Électra

Daughter of Agamemnon and Clytemnestra.

Clytemnestra

Queen of Argos who murdered her husband and married Aegisthus.

Aegisthus

Murderer of Agamemnon, Clytemnestra's second husband, usurper of the throne of Argos.

ACT ONE

Setting

A square in Argos. In the center stands a statue representing Jupiter as god of flies and death. Orestes has come back to Argos, accompanied by his tutor. They are asking for the way to Aegisthus' palace, but no one volunteers any information. Jupiter comes forward and explains that today is the Day of the Dead in Argos. It is the anniversary of Agamemnon's death. Agamemnon was a good ruler, Jupiter admits, but he had a great fault. He had forbidden that executions take place in public. That was a pity. Executions distract the people. The inhabitants of Argos were bored; they hungered for the spectacle of a violent death. When Agamemnon was killed, everyone kept silent. Orestes is indignant against the gods. Why have they permitted the assassin to enjoy fifteen years of happiness? Jupiter, offended, warns him not to blame the gods. They have turned the assassination to the profit of morality. They have sent down the flies on Argos. Then he adds that the flies are merely a symbol. To show what he means, he stops an old hag, and, seizing her by the scruff of the neck so that she cannot escape, asks her whom she is mourning.

She is wearing the national costume of Argos, she answers. That is, she is mourning Agamemnon. Jupiter asks her what she was doing while the King was being slain. Why, all she could do was to lock her door, she responds; her husband was away working. But she must have opened the window to hear better; that night she must have doubly enjoyed making love, Jupiter claims. She is repentant, the old hag replies apologetically, the whole family has been repenting ever since. Even her grandson, who is not yet seven years old, has been brought up in that spirit and is already imbued with the sense of original sin. Jupiter lets her go and she scurries off while the god remarks that he is satisfied with her conduct; her piety is solidly grounded in fear. In other words, the gods were right in letting Aegisthus reign. Orestes asks whether Aegisthus himself feels contrite. He would be surprised if he did, replies the god. But after all, the whole city is doing penance for him. Repentance is weighed by the pound.

The conversation veers to Orestes. According to some reports, Jupiter states, he was found and brought up by some rich Athenian citizen. Jupiter, who has been shadowing him for some time, exhorts Orestes to leave Argos (he still pretends that he does not know Orestes' identity) because the inhabitants of the city have taken the road of penance. Orestes' innocence separates them from him; he was not saturated by their sense of guilt, as he was not an accomplice in the murder. The people of Argos are afraid, and terror has a delectable odor to the gods.

Jupiter departs. The tutor himself urges Orestes to leave. Did he not teach him that one must never involve oneself; did he not liberate him from all superstitions? Orestes, he affirms, is the most enviable of mortals, having no beliefs, no family ties, no country, no religion, available to all experience, yet never engaging himself. He has given him a superb liberal education.

Comment

The tutor is expounding here the theory of availability (la disponibilité), advocated by André Gide (1869-1951), a writer who powerfully influenced young French intellectuals in the years between the two world wars. Sartre argues that it does not suffice to be free if one does nothing with one's freedom. His philosophy is one of involvement (l'engagement). The individual must take an active part in the life of society.

But Orestes yearns to belong somewhere. He has been an exile all his life. He needs memories of a land that he could call his own and of a house that he could call home. Yet this need was not fulfilled because Aegisthus palace was not really his own. If only he could perform an action, he says, by which he could establish himself in the memory of the people of Argos, he would do it if it meant killing his own mother.

Enter Électra. She has come to empty her trashcan, as she is wont to do, in front of the statue of Jupiter. She insults the god, unafraid, and voices her hope that one day her brother will return and avenge himself. She notices Orestes and although she does not yet know who he is, tells him that the Queen has her do the humiliating menial household chores. Clytemnestra herself appears. They hurl insults at each other; they also compete for Orestes' attention.

Comment

It is evident that Clytemnestra and Électra hate each other because of their similarity. Clytemnestra is an older image of her daughter, already burned out by passion. She hates her own fervent youth in her daughter.

The Queen tells Orestes that most travelers avoid Argos because of its ill fame. Électra immediately retorts that her mother is making a public exhibition of her guilt. Public confessions are the national game of the people of Argos.

Comment

Public self-accusation as a national pastime is a reference to the hearings held by the Pétain regime in 1940 to determine the responsibility for the fall of France.

But Clytemnestra answers that she does not regret Agamemnon's death: all she grieves for is her lost son whom Aegisthus handed over to his mercenaries. At the end of the first act Jupiter appears and offers Orestes a team of horses at an advantageous price if he wishes to leave town. But Orestes says that he has changed his mind; he is staying. Jupiter then extends his hospitality to Orestes. He will find lodgings for him at the inn where he is staying.

Comment

This play poses the same fundamental question that we have already faced in connection with *No Exit:* why does Sartre, an atheist, introduce the supernatural into his dramas? In fact, his Catholic critics, notably Henri de Lubac and Gabriel Marcel, have said that it is strange to see an atheist concern himself as frequently with problems of the divinity as Sartre does. The answer is that to Sartre God exists inasmuch as he lives in the imagination of the people. Jupiter here is a phantom, an idea represented by an actor, just as Prudence or Justice might be personified in a statue though they do not exist as concrete individuals. The gods of antiquity provide a particularly good subject for Sartre, because in mythology they appear as beings with whom one can argue and bargain, whom one can defy or cheat. In other words, they are obviously anthropomorphic. Sartre's conviction is that the concept of the divinity is used by the ruling classes to cow the people into submission.

ACT TWO, FIRST TABLEAU

Setting

The entrance to the cave of the dead. The opening itself is blocked by a stone. To the left are steps leading to a temple. The crowd has gathered to witness the arrival of the spirits of the dead. The stone will be rolled away from the cave which, according to popular belief, leads to the underworld. This is an annual event that has been celebrated at Argos, by order of Aegisthus, even since Agamemnon's assassination. Électra is missing, but Aegisthus commands that the celebration commence. Nothing is seen of the spirits, but Aegisthus announces them one by one to the crowd: here is the ghost of the husband of Aricia, the unfaithful wife; there is the mother of Nicias who died because her son did not take care of her old age; there come the spirits of all of Ségestes's debtors who died in destitution. The people cower in fear and horror; even the children cry out that they were not born on purpose and that they are ashamed of growing up. Aegisthus reminds them that his penance is the greatest, as he has to welcome Agamemnon's ghost. Orestes, outraged by this comedy, wants to interfere, but Jupiter restrains him. At this moment, Électra appears in a white dress. She refuses to mourn the dead in black, she declares. She is not afraid of them, as she is not guilty. While the crowd is shouting "sacrilege" at her, she summons the dead to show by some sign if her conduct displeases them. She starts to dance. Jupiter, still present in his disguise, murmurs some magic phrases and the stone rolls away by itself from the cave. Électra is not impressed, but the crowd is now convinced of her fault. Aegisthus, taking advantage of this event, tells her that she will have to leave Argos immediately and calls on the people to strike her down like an infected animal if they still find her in the city the next day at dawn. In the final scene Électra and Orestes are alone. Orestes tells her that he is her brother and urges her to flee Argos together with him; he is disgusted by all the blood that has been spilled. She refuses; she belongs to the dynasty of the Astrides; her place is right here. Orestes, undecided, prays to Zeus and asks him to indicate to him by a sign if he should depart from Argos. Jupiter, who has been lurking about in the background, readily obliges and produces another minor miracle: light streams out from behind the rocks. But it does not achieve its intended effect: Orestes, wondering if to be good means always to say "excuse me" and "thank you," departing by the back door, suddenly makes up his mind to stay and to claim his inheritance. He has become a man. He says that the wants to deserve the name of "thief of remorse"; that is, he will take upon himself all the guilt of the people of Argos. As the curtain falls, Orestes takes Électra protectively in his arms.

Comment

We have seen how adroitly Aegisthus exploits the fears and superstitions of his subjects. Of course, they are guilty: first, they were accomplices in Agamemnon's murder. Sartre shows the social implications of crime. We delegate some members of society to commit murder for the entire community. Aegisthus' act was not altogether an individual accomplishment but rather the expression of the malice of the community toward Agamemnon, a just ruler who had forbidden public executions.

Second, Aegisthus' subjects all had their own faults. His ingenuity lies in turning all this to his profit. He himself is not contrite in the least. He provides a classical example of the *salaud* in Sartre's dictionary. What is the significance of Orestes' decision to ask for a sign from Zeus? Sartre believes that there may be "signs" or phenomena that we might consider as such. However, he contends, actually we ourselves interpret these signs the way we want to. We are free, yet we constantly try to convince ourselves of the necessity of our actions. In real life, there is no Jupiter around to perform miracles, but the powers that be, the authorities, the leaders, have their own little tricks. It should be borne in mind that Jupiter in the play is only a second-rate magician: he cannot do anything about Orestes' decision to stay, since according to Sartre, no power can constrain us to obey against our will.

ACT TWO, SECOND TABLEAU

Setting

The throne room in the royal palace. Électra and Orestes enter stealthily. They hear the guards coming and hide behind the throne. The guards do not notice them. Aegisthus and Clytemnestra appear. Aegisthus says that the people were on the point of believing Électra when the miracle occurred. But he does not look forward to punishing the girl. He feels very tired. All the mourning has finally ruined his spirits. As the Queen leaves he continues to talk to himself. He is less alive than Agamemnon. He feels nothingness around him. Enter Jupiter. The god tries to comfort him: he is good for another twenty years. But Aegisthus is fed up with life. Jupiter reveals that Orestes is in the city and wants to kill him. Aegisthus has no intentions of having him arrested. But Aegisthus' rule is dear to Jupiter. His crime was nothing: Agamemnon, he says, was going to die of apoplexy three months later, anyway, and the murder was compensated by the repentance of twenty thousand souls. Gods and kings have a painful secret, Jupiter affirms. Men are free. Fortunately, they do not know it. Why, Aegisthus replies, if they knew it they would have long ago done away with him. He does not see much similarity between himself and the gods. Ever since the beginning of his reign, he has been at work creating an image of himself in his subjects and now he has been caught in his own trap: he sees himself as they look at him; he is nothing but the fear in his subjects' hearts. It is no different with gods, Jupiter claims; they too need their images. If he only forgot himself for a minute. . . He does not wish to talk about such an eventuality.

Comment

Sartre intimates here that if God were erased from the minds of the people, He would at that instant cease to exist, since according to the playwright, He is not a transcendent reality but a mere figment of the imagination.

Jupiter demands that Orestes be seized. But Aegisthus objects, why doesn't Jupiter strike him with a bolt of lightning if he thinks Orestes is doing harm? Once freedom has exploded in a man's soul, Jupiter explains, the gods can do nothing against him. Aegisthus halfheartedly agrees to have Orestes executed, but when the latter comes out of his hiding place, sword in hand, he puts up no resistance. His last words curse Orestes and warn him that the flies will not leave him alone. While Orestes goes to Clytemnestra's chamber, Électra remains on stage, listening to her mother's cries of agony. But when Orestes reappears, her sentiments begin to change. She rejects Orestes' assumption that they are now free. She is not free, she says, to undo all the horror they have caused. She now sees millions of eyes fixed at her: the Érinyes have come to claim their victim. Orestes leads her away to Apollo's sanctuary.

Comment

The constant references to death with relation to the city of Argos, and the King and Queen in particular, exemplify the state of affairs that sets in when people accept themselves as unchangeable, petrified essences. Aegisthus finds that he has become a prisoner of the image he has engendered in his subjects. They do not move forward; they keep wallowing in remorse and thereby they spare themselves the anguish of choice. The royal couple are dead in the sense that they merely live up to their destiny handed to them by Agamemnon's assassination. Aegisthus is the set image of penance, even though it is a false one. For Sartre, man without action is nothing. That is why Aegisthus is tormented by the concept of nothingness and is weary of life.

ACT THREE

Setting

The temple of Apollo. Électra and Orestes are asleep at the foot of the statue, surrounded by the Érinyes. When Électra awakens, she is afraid. She hardly recognizes Orestes. But Électra herself has changed. She strikingly resembles Clytemnestra. More and more, she tries to dissociate herself from Orestes and his crime. She is tempted to choose the road of repentance. In fact, Jupiter, arriving, offers her the throne of Argos and proposes that Orestes, too, return in the spirit of contrition. Opening up the ceiling of the temple, Jupiter shows him the planets circling on their paths, never colliding with one another, according to the principles of justice created by himself. The world is good, he says; he created it according to his will and he is the Supreme Good. Orestes has done evil, yet the evil he is so proud of is but a reflection of being, a deceptive image whose very existence is sustained by the Good.

Comment

Sartre here makes of Jupiter the mouthpiece of the Catholic Church. According to scholastic philosophy, evil is a privation, i.e., the lack of something that should exist. Thus a one-armed man suffers from physical evil. Whatever is, is good. To take an example of moral evil, lying would be considered as a lack of truthfulness.

Jupiter summons Orestes to return to the fold, the ways of nature. Orestes boldly answers that Jupiter is the god of stones and stars, but not of men; he created man, but gave him free will. Free will was intended to serve him, but it turned against him, and he is powerless against it, for if he constrained it to do as he bids the will would no longer be free. Orestes accepts and claims the terrible solitude of freedom. Freedom is exile; he is outside of nature, against it, without any given set of laws; for each man should invent his own path. But the price of freedom is too high for Électra. Despite her brother's entreaties she accepts the hand extended to her by Jupiter and runs away, saying that she feels repentant.

Orestes is now alone. But lo! the tutor rushes in, discontentedly picking his way among the Érinyes whom he considers a particularly unhealthy form of superstition. Orestes commands him to throw the gates wide open. Outside, the crowd of the inhabitants of Argos has gathered, crying for his blood. Orestes greets them, unafraid, as the rightful heir to the throne. The crime he committed, he says, is his own; but he killed in order to liberate them. They should no longer fear their dead. He claims the throne of Argos, but he will not occupy it. He wants to be a king without a land and without subjects. In parting, he tells them a fable. One summer, the town of Skyros was infested with rats. One day, a flute player came. He stood in the middle of the town and began to play, and all the rats swarmed around him. Then the flute player started walking; for a moment the rats hesitated, then they all flung themselves after the flute player who disappeared forever with all the rats. Orestes descends the steps of the temple and leaves, while the Érinyes swoop down on him.

Comment

Orestes at the end is one of the rare embodiments of a true Sartrean hero, the authentic man who acts in perfect good faith. He performs his act in despair and solitude, overcoming existential anguish, shouldering total responsibility for what he has done. But did not Aegisthus and the people of Argos acknowledge themselves responsible for their crimes? After all, they were ready to pay for it with repentance. But, Sartre alleges, their solution was a false one. We cannot expiate our sins, at least not by beating our chests and asking forgiveness. Only an action can undo another action; wearing sackcloth and sprinkling ashes on one's head are gestures, not actions. The play's message had a direct relevance to the situation in France when it was produced in 1943. Aegisthus' attitude corresponds to the one of the Vichy government where leaders professed themselves to be partially responsible for France's defeat, but their reaction was negative: they served the Germans. Sartre espoused the cause of the resistance which fought the Fuehrer's troops.

ANALYSIS OF SELECTED CHARACTERS

Orestes

We have pointed out that he represents the authentic person. He has taken upon himself the sins of the people; in this sense he is a Christ-figure. What is the significance of his being persecuted by the Érinyes? They do not really stand for his conscience as we generally interpret the term. He feels no remorse. He will not expiate his crime. Yet he takes its burden upon himself. What is this burden then? It consists of his con-science, that is, the internalized gaze of society upon him; of society which will always condemn him. Pirandello, the playwright from whom Sartre learned the most, says that conscience is a representative of the voice of society inside us, implanted in us. The Érinyes first appear as so many pairs of eyes, eyes that judge Orestes. He accepts living with them to the end of his life. But he will not be their ruler. Sartre detests leaders; he argues that we must make up our own minds. Leaders serve as a pretext for us, yet another means of shunning responsibility. Here Sartre departs from the legend, which has Orestes return to Argos after his acquittal by the Aeropagos.

Électra

She is like many of Sartre's young women figures: she rebels but lacks the stamina to shoulder the consequences. In the end she follows Jupiter, which signifies that she takes refuge in repentance. However, it would be a mistake to speak of her as a "weak character" in the conventional meaning of the phrase. According to Sartre, no one is weak or strong per se; "weakness" lies in masking one's freedom from oneself.

The Tutor

He is a comic figure, very much in the tradition of teachers as they appear in French literature. He is used mainly as a foil for Orestes: he is not an individual but rather an accessory in the "young-man-in-search-of-truth versus his well-meaning elders" relationship. He is a reincarnation of Pangloss, Candide's master of philosophy in Voltaire's classic story.

. . . .

INTRODUCTION

To facilitate the understanding of the play, it will be helpful to acquaint the reader first with its basic mechanism, that is, with the existential situation the author wishes to portray. *No Exit* describes an emotional merry-go-round in which each of the three characters loves one person, but his love must remain unrequited: Inès, being attracted to Estelle, is repulsed by her; Estelle would like to flirt with Garcin who does not care for her; Garcin needs Inès's friendship, while Inès despises him. Diagrammatically, this may be shown in the following manner:

These three persons are thrust upon one another, seemingly without any means of escape. Later, we shall examine whether their predicament is really unalterable or whether Sartre wants to illustrate by it a point that is in fact opposed to the surface meaning of the play.

CHARACTERS

Garcin

A middle-aged Brazilian journalist. He is politically oriented. His views are leftist; he expresses his ideas vehemently. He is intellectual, but not to the point of inactivity.

Estelle

An insane, pretty blonde, much younger than her partners. Her sole interest lies in cultivating her own attractiveness as a female.

Inès

A Lesbian of approximately Garcin's age, hardened by life, predatory and cruel.

Attendant

His only function is to usher in the other persons.

Setting: The stage shows a room furnished in the style of the Second Empire (Napoléon III, 1850-70). Furniture of this period is massive and ornamental. Its significance is that to Sartre it suggests middle-class values. The spectator soon realizes that the action does not take place in any ordinary room; he is looking at life hereafter. All the characters are dead, they are in hell. However, already at this point we must emphasize that Sartre does not believe in the immortality of the soul. Hell, here, is merely a literary device that Sartre uses allegorically to show life on earth.

PLOT STRUCTURE

Scenes One To Four

Garcin enters, followed by the attendant. He immediately realizes where he is (although he does not pronounce the word "hell"). First, he is looking for the instruments of torture, but then it strikes him that the torture he is going to be subjected to is of a subtler kind. For one thing, it consists in the presence of the drawing-room furniture, which reminds him of what he considers as bourgeois (upper-middle-class) ideals; for another, in perpetual consciousness (there is no sleep and he cannot close his eyes even to wink). The door will be locked at all times. There is a doorbell, but, he is told, it functions capriciously: at times it works, at times it does not. The attendant leaves. Garcin, suddenly gripped by fear, tries the bell. It is silent. He cries out for help. There is no answer. Shortly afterwards, the door opens and Inès appears, accompanied by the servant. Garcin rises to introduce himself, but Inès cuts him short, saying that she knows who he is: the tormentor. While Garcin protests, we feel that Inès, almost instinctively, has hit the nail on the head. She also notices that Garcin is afraid. Being unmoved and strong herself, she looks at him with contempt and rejects his advances.

Once more the door opens and Estelle is ushered in. She complains that the color of her couch clashes with her dress. Inès offers Estelle her own, but she turns it down, saying that only the gentleman's couch would go with her dress. Garcin, slightly annoyed, stands up, while Inès declares that she is delighted to make Estelle's acquaintance.

Comment

The circle is now complete. The perceptive reader has noticed by now that the participants had been trapped. Already they are involved with one another. Inès, a mature woman who is intelligent enough to understand Garcin, could be his salvation if she only listened; Estelle, the pretty little blonde, could make Inès happy, but she is not interested in her; Garcin, as a male, represents Estelle's potential salvation, but he knows that she is too vacuous to understand him. However, it is not only that each is spurned by the object of his or her love. At the same time, all of them must feel the condemning gaze of their enemies behind their backs. Inès realizes that she is watched by Garcin while trying to woo Estelle, and Estelle feels Inès' eyes upon her while flirting with Garcin. The gaze (le regard) of "the other" (any other human being) is one of the key terms in existentialist philosophy. In *Being and Nothingness,* Sartre says that the gaze of other people "steals my world" (that is, the world I have constructed for myself out of ideas I accept), because it reduces me to an object. In other words, one is convinced that one is the center of the universe until the appearance of another consciousness, which limits one's autonomy, because it too regards itself as a center, a subject (instead of an object), an end (rather than a means). It too has ideas about the universe that collide with my own. In this sense, the characters of *Huis-Clos,* rejecting one another, become each other's damnation. Yet the conclusion that "hell is other people" does not represent the deepest meaning of the play. To get to this, we must first resume the thread of the plot.

Scene Five

Estelle looks back on earth where they have just buried her. She says she died of pneumonia. The conversation now drifts to the question of why they locked up just the three of them together. Garcin thinks it was a mere coincidence, but Inès is skeptical. She is convinced that everything has been prearranged, they left nothing to chance, every detail serves some purpose. They now decide to tell about their lives in order to find out why they chose the three of them. Estelle starts. She says she has probably been chosen by error. She has nothing to hide. She was an orphan. An old friend of her father's had asked for her hand in marriage. He was a good man, and wealthy. She consented. For six years they had lived together peacefully. But two years ago Estelle met the man she was to love. He wanted them to elope, but she refused. After that she was struck by pneumonia. (We shall soon find out that she is not telling the complete truth about her past.)

Now it is Garcin's turn. He edited a pacifist paper. War broke out. He refused to compromise, continuing his intransigent line against the war. He was arrested and shot. (He too is lying, as it will turn out.) Inès, who suspects that both confessions presented a doctored version of the truth, discovers the real reason why they have been put in the same room: each of them is the torturer of the other two. They are stunned, recognizing the accuracy of her remark, not even venturing to contradict her. Then Garcin proposes that they defy the punishment intended for them: if they keep quiet, without getting involved in each other, they can thwart the intentions of the "management." But Estelle soon breaks the silence, complaining that she has no mirror. Inès volunteers that she will serve as a mirror for her. Estelle looks into Inès eyes but says that she sees herself very indistinctly. No matter how much Inès attempts to please her or cow her into submission, Estelle only uses her to attract Garcin's attention.

Comment

The mirror (le miroir) is another important word in the vocabulary of the French avant-garde (artistic innovators). It may mean an actual looking-glass, but by extension it is also used metaphorically (as an implicit comparison) to signify consciousness, more precisely the reflective character of consciousness. In our comment to scenes one to four of *No Exit,* we mentioned that the appearance of another human being reduces us to an object and for this reason we can never totally accept each other's presence. On the other hand, Sartre tells us, we nevertheless need each other, for we become more real to ourselves when we grasp ourselves as reflected in another person's mind. This may sound very esoteric, but it is simply an explanation of the phenomenon commonly called loneliness. When we have been cut off from human company, we yearn for it. We want to know what others think of the experiences we are undergoing. We wonder if they see us in the same way as we do. This is what is meant by our need of another consciousness as a mirror. When Estelle remarks that she does not see herself well in Inès' eyes this implies that she does not wish to be reflected by her because she rejects Inès as a human being. She only aspires to be known by Garcin. The question may arise, why can they not turn around and defy the "management," that is, God, if we want to interpret it that way, by starting to like each other in a mutual manner? This will be answered later.

Garcin tries to abide by his resolution not to speak, but Inès derides him, saying that she is aware of his hated presence every moment, whether he looks at them or not. She wants to choose her hell rather than pretend not to notice it. Garcin finally explodes under her needling and starts speaking again. Now he will tell the real reason why he has been sent to hell, he asserts. He had tortured his wife. She was a lamb-like creature who never reproached him for anything. He used to come home drunk, smelling of wine and women. Yet she suffered silently. Her submissiveness was a challenge to him to deceive her even more. This is still not what he feels to be the real cause of his damnation. (He is still hiding something).

Inès now decides to tell her story. Already on earth she was what people refer to as a "damned woman" (a Lesbian). She was living in an apartment with a male cousin and Florence, his wife. Inès hated him and gradually succeeded in making Florence see him through her (Inès') eyes. One day he was run over by a streetcar. (We are to understand that this was actually a form of suicide.) Inès and Florence took a room at the other end of town. But she did not cease to remind Florence that in fact it was they who killed her husband. In six months, she had destroyed Florence's resistance. Finally, one night Florence got up and turned on the gas. They were both asphyxiated.

Inès and Garcin ply Estelle with questions and presently she breaks down. She too is guilty. Her paramour wanted a child. She was against it, but she did become pregnant. It was a girl. Afraid of her husband she killed the baby, drowning her in the lake at which they were vacationing. Her paramour committed suicide out of despair. It was all for nothing, as her husband had actually never suspected her. Estelle, in turn, calls herself a coward.

As the play advances, little by little the earth fades away: they mention it less and less. Inès' room has been rented. A couple live in it now; she puts her hands on his shoulders, but Inès can no longer see exactly what is happening. At last the light goes out entirely. This means that she is no longer concerned with things on earth. Estelle goes through the same process. Now she is looking at a dance hall. Olga, one of her friends, is dancing the Saint Louis Blues with a young man of eighteen of whom

Estelle used to be very fond. They are acting very intimately. Estelle would like to take him away from her. But now Olga is talking to the young man. She tells him everything about Estelle: the vacation in Switzerland, the child, the murder. Now it is all finished. Estelle is no longer interested in the young man. she has severed her last ties with the world.

Inès makes another overture to Estelle. Estelle will shine in her gaze as a grain of gold in the sunlight. Her eyes will mirror Estelle the way she wants to be seen. Estelle desperately fights to escape from her grip and at last spits in her face. At this point, Garcin resolves to endeavor to make Estelle his partner. He must be understood on an intellectual level. (More than anything else he is a political animal; sex is a secondary consideration with him.) Therefore, he explains to her about his past activities. He wants Estelle to have absolute confidence in him. Estelle consents, though political questions bore her. He repeats that he was shot. However, it now becomes evident that he formerly gave a falsified story of the circumstances of his death. He did not exactly refuse to leave. As a matter of fact, he took the train to Mexico. He wanted to continue his work there. He wanted to serve as a witness. (Actually, he is trying to justify himself; one understands that he fled because he was a coward.) They caught him on the frontier and that is how he was shot. Now he would like Estelle to tell him whether he acted honorably or not. But Estelle listens to him unimpressed. How could she know? All she wants is Garcin's love. He continues to reason. What were his real motives, he asks himself. True enough, even at the last moment, he did not face death bravely. But that was merely because of a weakness of the body, not the mind. For Garcin, earth is still visible. His colleagues are thinking of him. They shake their heads and they say, "Garcin is a coward." If at least one person could have faith in him, he would leave hell. Estelle feebly insists that she does. But Inès, breaking out in sardonic laughter, asserts that Estelle would tell him anything to please him: all she wants is a man. Irked by Garcin's continual prodding, Estelle answers that she would love him even if she knew that he was a coward. Garcin again feels crestfallen. He has now given up as far as the other two are concerned. He will escape alone. In desperation, he starts banging on the door, shouting that he would rather endure anything than be locked up with these people. And lo and behold! the door opens. Garcin is dumbfounded. He does not leave. Neither do the others. Garcin closes the door.

It was for Inès' sake that he stayed, Garcin states. He can no longer change the views of the people on earth. Estelle does not count. He must convince Inès that he is not a coward. He never cared much for love or money, he admits. He wanted to be a man. Inès contemptuously objects that intentions do not count. A person is but the sum of his actions. She thinks he is a coward and that alone makes him one. Crouching before Inès' steady gaze, Garcin comes to the conclusion that "hell is other people." He picks up a paper knife and attempts to stab Inès, only to realize that his action is senseless-they are all dead. Exhausted, they fall back on their couches, gathering new strength for the next round of the comedy which they realize they will continue acting out forever.

Comment

We have already pointed out that Sartre, an atheist, does not believe in afterlife. What he considers to be the myth of hell serves for him, therefore, solely as a foil to exemplify his philosophical doctrine about life here and now. What, then, is the significance of this seemingly absurd carousel made up of three dead persons? We have emphasized that Sartre's philosophy is one of absolute freedom. He thinks of damnation as a condition in which our life lies before us all finished and we are unable to change anything about it. If such a place did exist, Sartre would argue, that would indeed be an inferno. Fortunately, he claims, this is not our lot. We always have choices to make, we are not imprisoned. Our past does not determine our actions in the present. In real life, Inès could choose to like Garcin; according to Sartre, there is no such thing as human nature or personality, that is, there exists no biological or psychological compulsion that would force Inès to be attracted to Estelle rather than Garcin. The same way, Garcin, where he still alive, would not have to contemplate incessantly his past to find out whether he is a coward; all he would have to do is to go out in the world and behave bravely, there would be nothing to prevent him from doing so. Sartre's main point in this play is therefore that many of us behave in life as though we were in hell-in fact, we choose our hell by pretending that we are the victims of circumstance, that we cannot change our nature, that we must act in one way or another because we have been so conditioned by past experience. Remember that when the door opens, none of the characters leave. This demonstrates that their condition is self-chosen. They have nowhere to go because they prefer their present miserable existence to the anguish that choice and the recognition of freedom would entail. Thus, many people go through life acting as if they were imprisoned. Sartre would say that Garcin's and Estelle's "sin" is that they comport themselves like cowards (laches). That is, instead of starting to perform courageous deeds, they prefer to accept themselves as such. Inès represents the other "sinful" type of conduct in Sartre's eyes: she is what he calls a "skunk" (salaude) in the sense that she pretends that all her actions were predetermined by some kind of supernatural power. This is why she is the one who always reminds the other two that everything has been taken care of, that they cannot outwit the "management." Thus, all three take refuge in the cocoons of their supposed personalities and are willing to continue the comedy of mutual recriminations and frustrations forever. Sartre's conclusion, therefore, is that we must change ourselves every day in dynamic action in order to avoid hell on earth (cf. *Bad Faith and Types of Erroneous Conduct* in the section on Existentialism).

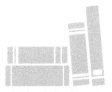

DIRTY HANDS

INTRODUCTION

Dirty Hands is a psychological whodunit. Its action is tautly woven; Sartre never allows the spectator's interest to flag. But, naturally enough, the author's aim is not merely to provide an entertaining evening for the audience: he has an ultimate purpose, a moral one, as usual. As in conventional detective stories, we must find out the identity of the murderer; however, this word is not to be taken in its police-file meaning. We know that Hugo Barine killed Hoederer; the question is, which Hugo did it: was it Hugo the traitor, Hugo the jealous husband, Hugo the rebellious son or Hugo the revolutionary? In other terms, we must find out the reason for his action. The play investigates the motivation of a significant human act in the light of all the evidence and thereby attempts to illustrate one of the axial tenets of Sartre's philosophy.

MAIN CHARACTERS

Hugo

A twenty-one-year-old intellectual rebel, son of a wealthy industrialist.

Jessica

Hugo's wife. She has largely accepted the social position of women in European society. She is pretty and sophisticated, but does not face reality enough to fulfill her husband's aspirations.

Hoederer

One of the leaders of Illyria's proletarian party, a man of great personal magnetism.

Louis

Leader of an opposing faction in the same Party, Hugo's superior.

Olga

Hugo's collaborator. She loves Hugo but puts her allegiance to the Party before her emotions toward him.

Karsky

Head of the liberal bourgeois movement in Illyria. His party has been outlawed by the present government.

The Prince

Son of Illyria's present ruler. His father, the Regent, is a fascist and governs the country autocratically.

Slick And George

Hoederer's bodyguards, animal types.

Time and setting of action: We are in the country of "Illyria." This was the name Napoléon gave to his Balkan provinces. Sartre chose it to indicate that the play takes place somewhere in the Balkans. The conditions described suggest those in Rumania, Bulgaria and Yugoslavia during the Second World War. The first and last acts occur in 1945, while the rest of the drama provides a flashback to two years earlier. The stage shifts from Olga's modest home in acts one and two to Hoederer's more substantial residence in acts three to six and then back to Olga's room in act seven. The acts are termed tableaux in the original French, as they comprise series of scenes acted in one setting.

ACT ONE

Hugo, suddenly release before time from prison, appears at Olga's apartment. She hesitates, but then opens the door for him. He notices Olga's mixed emotions upon seeing him. Hugo does not yet know that the party line has changed since his imprisonment and Hoederer is no longer regarded as having been anti-party. Under these circumstances, he is only in the way as Hoederer's assassin. He tells Olga that while in prison he received some chocolates sent by an unknown person and accidentally found out that the chocolates were poisoned. He is convinced that it was the Party that had decided that he should die but has not yet learned the real reason for it. He suspects, too, that they will send someone after him to put him out of the way. They know that he talks too much and is too dangerous, now that he is at liberty. (Hugo was ordered by Louis, his superior in the Party, to kill Hoederer, but this has been kept secret.) If fact, someone is already at the door and

Hugo barely has time to slip into the adjoining room. They have come to get Hugo, just as he has foreseen. Olga does not deny that Hugo is in her bedroom, but she asks that his case be examined. Perhaps he can be rehabilitated and made to become useful once again to the Party. The circumstances of Hoederer's murder have never been completely cleared up. Some say that he only killed Hoederer for some private motive, perhaps jealousy. That is, he is not a dependable party worker but merely an amateur, a muddle-headed young intellectual. Olga presently obtains a three-hour reprieve for Hugo. She is going to question him thoroughly about his motivation in the murder and after three hours she will tell the comrades who came to liquidate him whether the verdict is "guilty" or "innocent," whether his life should be spared or taken. The following acts comprise a flashback, as Hugo now tells his story to Olga.

Comment

Ironically, the leader of the group that comes to liquidate Hugo is Louis, the same person who gave him the assignment to assassinate Hoederer. The playwright wished to show here the absurd fluctuations in Communist policy under Stalin's rule. This policy sacrificed principles as well as individuals when it was judged politically expedient. The Party is never actually referred to as the Communist Party, but the author leaves no doubt that this is meant. Moreover, circumstances in Illyria parallel those existing in France during the Vichy regime, 1940-1944.

ACT TWO

The time is March 1943, and the locale is still Olga's apartment. Hugo has now been in the Party for one year. He joined when the Regent of Illyria had declared war against the Soviet Union. But other factors in his background also become apparent. He detests his father. He professes to love his wife, Jessica, but nevertheless is weary of life. He has been entrusted with editing the Party's newssheet, but he would like a more dangerous assignment. Presently, Louis enters and tells Olga and Hugo that he is greatly mortified by what Hoederer is planning to do. The Regent, who knows that the military situation of the Axis powers is hopeless, wants to come to an understanding with the Party. After the war the Regent's own fascist government would share the power with a liberal bourgeois group called the Pentagon, and the Party of the proletariat, Hugo's Party. Hoederer is in favor of this, and his influence is so great that he has secured the votes of four of the seven members on the Party's executive committee. Louis is the leader of the faction opposing any such agreement. He says that Hoederer must be eliminated; once he is gone, the rest of the committee will no longer resist Louis's faction. Louis wants Hugo to serve as an informer. Hoederer needs a secretary and Hugo will be sent to his house in this capacity. But Hugo does not want to be a mere spy: he offers to murder Hoederer himself, without anyone's help. With some reluctance, Louis, who does not completely trust Hugo, accepts the latter's proposition. At this moment, an explosion is heard: another young revolutionary has just succeeded in carrying out a dangerous assignment. Hugo regards this as a good omen.

Comment

Hugo's world-weariness, his death wish (his assignment is a suicidal one) are to be attributed to his high sensitivity, his analytical mind, his incapacity to reach decisions. Joining the Party was the first defiant gesture in his life, an expression of hatred toward his energetic, aggressive father who overshadowed his childhood. His relationship with his wife is not totally satisfactory either. They seem to be children at play rather than man and wife. His marriage has not brought about a sense of fulfillment in Hugo.

ACT THREE

Hugo and Jessica have moved in at Hoederer's. While in each other's company, the two young people are playing a sophisticated game of make-believe: they imagine themselves in various roles. They mix fact and fancy. During the game Hugo tells her that he is going to kill Hoederer; she takes this up as an interesting idea and further elaborates on it. Offended in his vanity, Hugo now tries to convince her that he is serious about it. The roles they are acting out and the roles they really play in life become so entangled that the spectator cannot tell whether Jessica believes her husband or not. At any rate, she knows that he has acquired a revolver. Slick and George, Hoederer's bodyguards, now enter with the intention of searching the new arrivals. Hugo refuses.

They almost come to blows, but at last agree to call Hoederer to let him decide if a search is necessary. Hoederer appears. He wants to reconcile them. The bodyguards hate Hugo because he comes from a well-to-do family, because he has never known what it means to go without food; socialism is nothing but a theory with him. Hugo bitterly confesses that he has never succeeded in making the poor like him. All his efforts, all his good will have been in vain. Hoederer at last brings about a truce between them. Hugo is still adamant about the search, thinking that the revolver is in his suitcase, but Jessica offers to have the room searched. They do this, and find nothing. Finally Jessica, laughing, asks the bodyguards to search her too. Becoming self-conscious, the men hardly dare touch her. She has had the weapon on her all the time, having removed it from the suitcase without Hugo's knowledge.

The bodyguards depart. Hoederer noticed Hugo's fear while Slick and George were conducting their investigation. Warily he looks about, opens Hugo's suitcase and finds a number of photographs showing Hugo as a child. Thinking now that Hugo's apprehension was caused by the personal nature of these photos, i.e., it would have been embarrassing to have the guards discover his romantic attachment to his past, Hoederer leaves, satisfied of Hugo's innocence. At the end of the act Hugo succeeds in taking back the revolver from Jessica.

Comment

The incident of the photographs indicates Hugo's narcissistic tendencies, as well as the fact that he has not been able to move beyond his childhood problems. They still represent the overriding considerations in his present life. He needs to have his childhood image about him, because it reminds him of his frame of reference. His actions are reactions.

ACT FOUR

It seems now as though Hugo has started to vacillate in his determination to kill Hoederer. He has been captivated by Hoederer's personal charisma. He tells Jessica that Hoederer lends an aspect of reality to everything around him. Since Hoederer has taken him into his confidence, Hugo wonders if he will be able to shoot him.

Karsky, head of the liberal bourgeois party, and the Prince arrive on a secret mission. The Prince proposes the forming of a supreme council on which he is willing to give the proletarian party two votes out of twelve. Hoederer in turn states his conditions: he wants three out of six votes on the council, the other three to be distributed between Karsky and the Regent as they please. Knowing the Hoederer has behind him the might of the advancing Soviet armies, the Prince is ready to accept, and even the reluctant Karsky is forced to consider Hoederer's proposition. Hugo, outraged by Hoederer's willingness to collaborate with his enemies, interrupts the negotiation, but at this moment a detonation shakes the walls: a hand grenade has been thrown at the house. Hoederer is unhurt; he goes upstairs with the Prince and Karsky to continue their negotiations.

Hugo realizes the implication of this attempt on Hoederer's life. Louis and the other comrades who gave him his assignment no longer trust him and have now decided to deal with Hoederer in another fashion. Hugo is in despair. He drinks heavily and starts to intimate in front of the guards that he has a secret mission. To save the situation, Jessica tells the guards that the "secret" he mentioned is that she is going to have a child. Sarcastically, Hugo takes up the idea of himself as a family man. That would make something out of him. He would be someone who could be recognized, by the air of respectability on his face, by a certain taste in his mouth. But, he continues, that too would be a comedy. A family man is never a real family man; assassins are counterfeit assassins. Only the dead are for real. Everything else is make-believe, including what he is saying now. He is playing the comedy of despair. He invites the guards to shoot at him to deliver him from the torment of existence. Unless even the dead are impostors who play at being dead. At the end of the scene he collapses and the guards take him to his room.

Comment

The last scene of the fourth act is one of the most important in the play. Hugo's monologue has obvious overtones of Hamlet. In fact, Hugo as a character may be regarded as a twentieth-century version of the Danish prince. He, too, is tortured by the **metaphysical** problem of existence, but in a modern context. With him the question is posed less in terms of life or death, although he is contemplating murder, than as a failure in totally grasping reality. This provides one of the classic illustrations of the main doctrine in Sartre's ontology: the failure of the being-for-itself (l'être pour-soi) to resemble being-in-itself (l'être en-soi). Man, who is essentially consciousness, cannot attain the impenetrability, the "density" of lifeless matter. Man is not simply what he is, Sartre maintains, but only the consciousness of something, and he can never be equated with his object. To him, man is not a psycho-physical organism but a mental process. This process is one of continuous absorption, as the mind indeed incessantly aims at grasping, understanding, assimilating reality. When Hugo states that a family man is not entirely a family man, or that an assassin is never fully an assassin, he means that these concepts are static, they are taken from an external point of view, whereas man to himself is constant change, imitation, a project. For a fuller treatment of this **theme** see the section on *Being and Nothingness*.

ACT FIVE

Olga has come to pay a clandestine visit to Hugo. She detonated the hand grenade that missed Hoederer. She made the attempt in order to save Hugo's honor in front of the other comrades. She told no one that she was going to try to take Hoederer's life herself. All those in Louis's faction now think that Hugo is a traitor. Eight days have passed and nothing has happened. Hugo passionately affirms his determination to carry out his mission. Olga gives him twenty-four hours to do so and departs. Hoederer, suffering from insomnia and desiring human company, now comes to the room Hugo and Jessica are sharing. The subject of political compromise inevitably crops up and Hoederer makes an impassioned defense of his readiness to do business with the enemies of the Party. He affirms that the end always justifies the means; he will enter into a coalition with the fascists and the bourgeois liberals if he can save lives with it and secure advantages by it. Principles do not count. He loves people as they are, with all their rubbish and all their vices. Hugo, he says, is an anarchist who only wants to destroy, who hates others because he hates himself, whose purity resembles the perfection of death.

Comment

Hoederer's great attraction for people in general and Hugo in particular is that he is a man of action. Constantly vacillating and questioning, Hugo cannot achieve authenticity. Hoederer, on the other hand, transforms himself into pure action, so to speak. On the basis of his professed moral philosophy, Sartre could blame Hoederer's personal conduct only inasmuch as he did not fully realize his responsibility. (See Responsibility in the section on Existentialism.) He is better than the Prince or Karsky, who exhibit no trace of social conscience, yet his facility in action is attributable to the fact that he does not feel fully responsible for the consequences. The title of the play, *Dirty Hands*, has a certain relevance here. Hoederer's hands are admittedly soiled; this is the only way one can subsist in the world of practical politics. Sartre implies that Hugo's purity, his devotion to principle's, leads to sterility, even though his plight as a human being is worthy of compassion and even though it is the Hugos of this world who from time to time sacrifice themselves for a greater ultimate good. But no one is completely innocent in this play. As Hoederer says, we are all half accomplices, half victims.

Act Six

Next morning, Jessica insists on seeing Hoederer in his office. She lets him know that Hugo intends to murder him. Hoederer shows no surprise; he has known it since yesterday. Jessica warns him that Hugo will have his revolver on him when he comes in for work. She asks to have him disarmed, as she wants neither him nor Hoederer to be hurt. Hoederer is against disarming Hugo. He does not want to humiliate him. He is confident that Hugo is too intellectual to be able to carry out a murder mission. It is worth taking this chance, he contends, to gain Hugo's confidence. Jessica leaves by the window when they hear Hugo approaching.

Enter Hugo. In the dialogue that follows, Hoederer successfully convinces Hugo that he is not the type for committing murder. Hugo argues that he feels superfluous, that he is a nuisance to everyone, that no one loves him. Turning his back toward Hugo, Hoederer gives him a chance to shoot him. Hugo puts his hand in his pocket, hesitates. Hoederer turns around and takes the revolver from him, throwing it on his desk. He tells Hugo that he will help him. He will make a man out of the young rebel. Hugo has talent for writing. A good journalist serves the cause better than an unsuccessful assassin. When Hugo leaves, Jessica comes back through the window. Hoederer wants to send her away, but Jessica stays and makes an implicit declaration of love to Hoederer who, she realizes, is a true flesh-and-blood man. Hoederer objects: does she not love her husband? No, she answers, they are too much alike to love each other. She only feels like giggling when Hugo kisses her. Tempted, Hoederer kisses Jessica. At that moment, the door opens and Hugo appears on the threshold.

That was Hoederer's reason for sparing his life, Hugo concludes: he wanted Jessica to be around. Jessica protests, but Hugo interrupts her. He is not jealous, he says, since they never loved each other. He ironically recalls Hugo's phrase about helping him to become a man. Now he suddenly feels light and sure of himself. He picks up the revolver from the desk and shoots Hoederer three times. The guards rush in, but Hoederer tells them not to touch Hugo. He was jealous. "He thought I was sleeping with his wife," Hoederer says. Then, murmuring to himself that it was all an absurd misunderstanding, Hoederer dies.

Comment

It was a mistake on Hoederer's part to assume that Hugo was just not capable of murder. Let us remember that Sartre believes in total freedom. There is actually no such thing as "a murderer" or "a coward" in the absolute sense. In the scene with Jessican, Hugo realized that he was free. He overcame the anguish that characterizes the state in which we weigh several possible courses of action. Thus Hoederer has liberated Hugo; he has helped him to become a man as he promised, but this cost him his life. Now Hugo is something because he has performed a significant deed, he has left a trace in history as Hoederer's assassin.

ACT SEVEN

We are back in Olga's apartment. The time is again 1945. Hugo has now given an account of the circumstances of the murder. At the time he was entering Hoederer's study, he was going to tell Hoederer that he was ready to work with him. When he saw Jessica's lipstick on Hoederer, he suddenly knew that he was going to kill him. It was not that he was jealous of her. Rather, his trust in Hoederer was shaken; it seemed that Hoederer had betrayed him. Yet it was all pure chance. If he had opened the door two minutes earlier or two minutes later, he would not have murdered him. There were plenty of reasons for killing Hoederer: loyalty to Louis's group, belief in principles, feeling cheated on a personal level. But none of these provide an explanation of the action. Olga is now hopeful that Hugo can be "rehabilitated" for the Party.

But she must explain the present state of affairs. When the decision to liquidate Hoederer was reached, communications had broken down between Moscow and Illyria. As it turned out, Stalin would have approved of Hoederer's intention to enter into a coalition with the Regent. All of Hoederer's conceptions have now been vindicated and accepted as the official line of the Party. The comrades were told that Raskolnikoff (Hugo's underground name) worked for the Germans and assassinated Hoederer on orders from the Nazis. Hugo feels outraged. His action was for nothing, the Soviet Union decided to temporize with the enemy, the Party has three votes in the six-member council as Hoederer demanded. While he does not know why he killed Hoederer, he is convinced that he had to be killed, because his politics were bad. Olga, who loves him, tries to save him, but he refuses. He will not let his act sink into the morass of political stratagems. He will assume full responsibility for it. He opens the door to his butchers who are waiting for him outside, shouting "non recuperable" (cannot be redeemed).

Comment

As we have seen, the identity of the culprit cannot be established. *Dirty Hands* is a mystery play without a solution, for it is concerned with the mystery of free choice. Sartre has shown us the principal motives that psychologists would claim might explain the murder. Hugo revolted against paternal authority, his social conscience was moved by the misery of the proletariat, he owed allegiance to Olga, Louis and those who entrusted him with the mission, he felt hurt because Hoederer appeared to have betrayed his confidence. Sartre definitely eliminates only one possible motive, Hugo's love for Jessica. Jessica is now living with her father, and she and Hugo no longer even correspond. All these are equally good reasons, but they did not determine Hugo's action. He could have acted otherwise, he is responsible for what he did. At the end Hugo Barine realizes that Olga, Louis, and Hoederer were different from him: they belonged to the category of leaders. They are sure of themselves, because they claim to have been put at their posts by some predetermined order. They never falter, because they have no imagination. They are always in the right, because they never question themselves, they never ask what they owe to others. The end of the drama contains a powerful vindication of Hugo's position which has now achieved authenticity.

THE ROADS TO FREEDOM

THE AGE OF REASON (L'AGE DE RAISON)

....

INTRODUCTION

Many outstanding French writers have cultivated the novel cycle as a **genre**. Balzac, Zola, Proust, Roger Martin du Gard and Jules Romains have each channeled the main purport of their artistic and ideological message through the medium of one monumental fictional edifice. In these, every volume may usually be read as a separate novel, while the whole is intended to provide a panorama of the entire society or class in which the author lived. Sartre projected *Roads to Freedom* to be such an encyclopedic enterprise-one that would show the manner in which people choose their "selves" under such strains and tensions as existed preceding and during the Second World War. In *Roads to Freedom,* as in most cyclic novels, minor characters emerge to play important roles in later volumes and major ones sometimes disappear, never to be seen again. Of the three volumes published, *The Age of Reason* was a postwar sensation; it is the one that most closely follows the pattern of a traditional novel, in both style and scope, and is probably the most successful artistically as well in illustrating Sartrean theory.

THE AGE OF REASON (L'AGE DE RAISON)

In the early summer of 1938, Mathieu Delarue, aged thirty-four, a professor of philosophy at the Lycée Buffon in Paris, pays a visit to his mistress, Marcelle Duffet. Marcelle leads a secluded existence: she has few friends and almost never leaves her room in the house she shares with her mother. During their meeting, Mathieu learns that Marcelle is expecting a child. As he has no intention of marrying her, he takes it for granted that she too wants an abortion and Marcelle does not have the strength to object. She tells him that she has the address of a midwife who performs abortions. Mathieu goes to see the midwife, but her place turns out to be unsanitary, and he decides to consult Sarah, a mutual friend.

Boris Serguine, an ex-student of Mathieu's, is having an affair with Lola Montero, a middle-aged night-club singer. Boris has aspirations toward purity, but he cannot resist Lola and again sleeps over at her apartment. Lola is clinging to him desperately, for she feels old age approaching.

At Sarah's place, Mathieu finds Brunet, a Communist. Sarah's husband, Gomez, is fighting with the Loyalists against Franco in Spain and word has just arrived that he has become a colonel. Sarah informs Mathieu that she knows a doctor who handles abortion cases, a Viennese Jew on his way to the United States from Austria. Leaving Sarah, Mathieu crosses the Luxembourg Gardens and reflects on his frustrations. He no longer loves Marcelle, who has been his mistress for seven years. Unlike Brunet or Gomez, he had never involved himself in anything, and now it is too late to do so.

Mathieu is sitting with Ivich, Boris' sister, at a cafe table on Boulevard St. Michel. Mathieu is attracted to this unpredictable girl. Ivich is not doing well at school. She dreads going back to live with her parents at provincial Laon. Mathieu is called to the telephone: Sarah has found the Viennese doctor. He is asking 4,000 francs for the operation. Mathieu decides that he is going to borrow the money from Daniel, and leaves with Ivich to visit a gallery.

Meanwhile, Daniel Sereno has shaved, contemplating his handsome face in the mirror with disgust, barely overcoming the desire to disfigure himself with a cut. He puts his most prized possessions, his three cats, into a basket and takes a bus to the Seine with the intention of drowning them in the river. However, upon arriving he feels faint, cannot bring himself to kill the cats, and hails a cab to return home. He finds Mathieu in front of his door. Mathieu tells him that Marcelle is pregnant. Daniel feels like exploding in laughter, but masters himself and when Mathieu asks him to lend him 5,000 francs he refuses, claiming that he has lost all his money on the stock market.

Comment

What is the explanation for Daniel's whimsical actions? He wants to cut himself and resolves to drown the cats he is fond of with the sole purpose of hurting himself. Daniel belongs to the race of Sartrean characters who, in order to feel their existence more keenly, constantly punish themselves. To prove that he is unique and different from others, Daniel has become a homosexual. His malicious joy on learning that Marcelle is pregnant is due to his hatred for heterosexual relations. Now Mathieu may have to marry Marcelle and thereby become a family man, a respectable, righteous bourgeois. He refuses to lend him the money because he detests Mathieu's normalcy and does not mind his being in trouble.

Mathieu drops in at his brother Jacques's in order to borrow the necessary amount from him. Jacques is a successful lawyer. He refuses because he condemns Mathieu's loose life and welcomes the opportunity to humiliate him. Returning home, Mathieu has a long conversation with his friend Brunet who urges him to join the Communist cause. Though Mathieu feels that the Communists are on the right side in the Spanish Civil War, he argues that it would be insincere to identify himself with the party to the extent of becoming a card-carrying member.

Daniel walks down rue Réaumur and directs his steps to the seedy shooting gallery where he has previously made the acquaintance of unemployed youths. He tells himself that he only wants to see the desperate game going on between the "cruising" pederasts and the emaciated adolescents hoping to be picked up. He watches a middle-aged gentleman striking up a conversation with a youth and, breathing vengeance, he is ready to swoop down on them, pretending to be a detective, when he is approached by Bobby, one of his acquaintances. Frustrated in his determination to expose the pair, Daniel leaves, but not before he has learned the new address of Bobby and his friend, Ralph. Boris, Mathieu's ex-student, is in a bookstore, trying to steal a dictionary. He does this not because he needs the book or money but out of a thirst for adventure and danger. Just as he reaches for the dictionary, he feels a hand on his shoulder: it is Daniel Sereno. Daniel, who already knows Boris superficially, would like to talk to him, but he notices that Boris is not particularly anxious to converse with him. Daniel ascribes this to Mathieu's influence: he suspects that Mathieu warns his students about him. The truth is, however, that Boris wants to steal the book and knows that he must act now, as the store is going to close in a few minutes. Daniel coldly bids good-bye to Boris and leaves, furious with Mathieu. Boris succeeds in lifting the dictionary.

Daniel calls at Marcelle's. Mathieu does not know he has been functioning as Marcelle's confidential friend and adviser. He gets Marcelle to admit she would like to keep the baby. He offers to talk to Mathieu in order to convince him that he must marry Marcelle and legitimize their child. Daniel does this to wreak vengeance on Mathieu, thinking that the latter would lose his aura in front of his students if he became a married man.

Mathieu meets Ivich and Boris at the Sumatra, a night club where Lola Montero sings. Mathieu reveals to Boris his financial plight. Boris would like to help out Mathieu and asks Lola for 5,000 francs, not telling her what it is for. When Lola refuses, they get into an argument. Feeling dejected, Lola takes an overdose of the barbiturate she habitually uses to calm her nerves. Mathieu plunges a knife in his hand to impress Ivich. Next morning, Mathieu sees Ivich at the Café Dôme. She will know the result of her examination at two p.m. She suspects that she has failed and would do anything to avoid having to go back to Laon. She entertains the idea of becoming a saleswoman in a department store. Boris appears, looking white as a sheet, and collapses in a chair. Lola is dead, he says. Piecing the story together, Mathieu realizes that Lola took her barbiturate three times last night. Boris is also terrified because he had procured cocaine for Lola at various times in the past and his letters, in which he mentions these cocaine purchases, are in Lola's room. He knows that as soon as the police discover Lola's body they will find the incriminating letters.

Since Boris appears immobile, Mathieu feels that he must go himself to retrieve the letters, and he takes a taxicab to her hotel. He finds Lola lying inert in her room and he too thinks she is dead. While looking for the letters, he discovers a wad of thousand-franc notes. He is tempted to take some of the money, but cannot bring himself to do it. However, he returns from the hall to prove that he is not too weak to steal. Lola has awakened from her stupor, her eyes are open. She asks Mathieu what has happened, and he answers that Boris thought she had died. As Boris was too dazed to act, he came over himself, Mathieu explains. Lola says she only has a headache and affirms that the effect of the dose will wear away soon. Mathieu leaves with Boris's letters in his pocket.

Returning to the cafe, Mathieu throws the letters on the table and tells the siblings that Lola is alive and is suffering merely from the aftereffects of the drug. Boris is none too relieved. He cannot bear the thought of looking at Lola again, he claims, after having thought of her as dead. To save the situation, Mathieu leaves a message at Lola's night club, to the effect that Boris will see her tomorrow. As the hours pass, Ivich's apprehension about the examination is increasing. Boris sees her home and, as Ivich is panic stricken, at one thirty he leaves for the university alone to learn the results.

Comment

Boris and Ivich Serguine are somewhat reminiscent of Hugo and Jessica in *Dirty Hands*. The latter were introduced as man and wife but, as we pointed out, actually resemble a brother-and-sister team. Like Hugo and Jessica, they understand each other thoroughly. They are intelligent, cynical and at times cruel. Their fast, sophisticated existence, their disdainful attitudes, their arbitrary and yet obstinate views appear to fascinate Mathieu (and Sartre). He would like to penetrate into their secret, shared world of exclusive intimacy. They are all the more exciting as types as they are the children of Russian emigres who belonged to the nobility. Sartre would refuse to admit to snobbery, yet high birth and great wealth often exercise a spell on him.

Daniel, who sent a special delivery letter asking Mathieu to see him, receives his friend at his apartment. He discloses to the incredulous Mathieu that he has been seeing Marcelle regularly and up to now they have preferred to keep these visits secret. Mathieu believes him only when Daniel produces a note from Marcelle in which he is referred to as "the archangel" (she regards Daniel as a trusted counselor). By subtle hints Daniel tries to persuade Mathieu that Marcelle wants to keep the child and intimates that the best solution would be to marry her. After Mathieu has left, Daniel rings up Marcelle to tell her that he did what he could to convince Mathieu and hopes that he will ask for her hand in marriage. She is deeply moved and feels grateful to Daniel. Mathieu tries to borrow from an institution where they give short-term loans at exorbitant rates. Mathieu is ready to sign anything, but he gives up when he learns that it would take another fortnight to get the money. The Jewish doctor is leaving for America in a few days. At his apartment, Mathieu receives a telegram from Ivich, informing him that she has failed her exam. He sets out to find her and finally comes upon an intoxicated and incoherent Ivich. She hates the thought of returning to live with her parents at Laon. Mathieu wants her to come back to Paris in October to try to pass her exams again. If her parents will not give her money after this year's failure, he will be able to provide for her. Ivich first refuses, then, when she is on the point of accepting, learns about Marcelle's pregnancy and presently rejects Mathieu's offer with an air of finality. She will not return to Paris at all, she says.

Daniel has gone to see Ralph, a youth with whom he has had sexual relations in the past. After the act is over, a sense of boundless disgust prevails over him. At home he tries to cut himself with his razor but does not have the strength. He runs off to a bar where he is suddenly struck by an idea that, he hopes, may save him.

In the meantime, Mathieu has slipped back to Lola's hotel room and stolen the money. He triumphantly takes it to Marcelle, and is surprised to find that Marcelle shows no gratitude. Hopefully, Marcelle asks if he has talked to Daniel. Then, suddenly sensing that Mathieu shirks from marrying her, Marcelle accuses him of no longer loving her. Mathieu, instead of beating around the bush, admits the truth of this statement. Marcelle throws the money in Mathieu's face and he leaves, humiliated.

Mathieu finds Ivich in his apartment. She is contrite: she apologizes for her brusqueness in rejecting Mathieu's help. She promises that she will return to Paris in the fall. She is fond of Mathieu but she does not love him, she tells him.

Comment

Mathieu's emotions toward Ivich are not easy to decipher. She is undoubtedly the person who means the most to him, yet he often hates her and is often indifferent to her. Sartre manages to render this strange relationship convincing despite the fact that, conforming with his theory, he does not treat love as an elemental affective storm but as a mode of conduct that must be revivified by successive choices.

Lola breaks in, imparting the news of the disappearance of the 5,000 francs. Lola is convinced that Boris took the money. While Ivich departs, Mathieu tries to prove that it was he who stole the banknotes. He needed the money desperately, he explains, and has every intention of giving it back to her. Daniel Sereno, who has probably been observing the scene through the keyhole, appears at this moment and hands over the 5,000 francs to Lola in an envelope. She recognizes the banknotes by the fragrance of her perfume. However, she is not satisfied, for she is more vexed by Boris's failure to see her than by the loss of the money. She asks Mathieu whether he thinks that Boris will return to her. Mathieu gives an affirmative answer and Lola goes off, not knowing what the future holds for her. When the two friends remain alone, Daniel discloses to Mathieu that he, Daniel, is going to marry Marcelle. Mathieu assumes that Daniel is in love with Marcelle but Daniel denies having any sentimental attachment to her. He is, he confesses, a pederast. Why is he then going to marry? Mathieu divines the truth when he suggests that Daniel wants to punish himself. Daniel affirms that he is going to be a model husband, asks Mathieu not to get in touch with him in the future and takes his leave. Alone in his study, Mathieu reflects that all his friends have abandoned him and concludes with some **irony** that he has now attained the age of reason.

Comment

In *The Age of Reason* world affairs stay in the background of the action. The Spanish Civil War and the Anschluss (the annexation of Austria by Hitler) are mentioned, but politics on the whole do not directly affect the lives of the principal characters. Brunet is the only person whose passionate interest centers around political questions.

The Age of **Reason** is a fine realistic novel. Sartre took pains to abide by his principles laid down in Qu'est-ce-que la littérature? (What is Literature?), published in *Situations II*, where he contended that the modern author must respect the relativity proposition, i.e., everything must be presented as it appears from the viewpoint of the characters, and no intrusion should be allowed by the omniscient narrator.

The most consistent application of this theory would involve the exclusive use of the stream-of-consciousness technique. In this volume, Sartre only occasionally resorted to a strictly stream-of-consciousness approach. For most of the time the story is told in the third person and in the past tense, by the impersonal narrator. The contention that the author should remain impersonal is not a new one; it was propounded by Flaubert and other realists well before the turn of the century. However, we should regard the absence of the omniscient narrator more as a literary device than a truly significant change in the nature of the modern novel. To be sure, the ideas are still Sartre's, and in the great majority of cases the author stacks the cards in such a way that the reader is allowed to reach only one conclusion. Sartre does not intrude to point out the foibles and shortcomings of the characters, yet the attentive reader can usually tell about each of them whether Sartre sympathizes with them or disapproves of them from personal as well as philosophical motives.

THE ROADS TO FREEDOM

THE REPRIEVE (LE SURSIS)

....

Comment

The action of the second volume takes place three months later, in September 1938, and encompasses eight days. The "reprieve" is a reference to the Munich Pact, the agreement between Chamberlain, Daladier, Hitler, and Mussolini that resulted in a year's postponement of the war, at the price of the partial dismemberment of Czechoslovakia. Chamberlain returned from Munich waving his umbrella, forecasting "peace for our time". As the clouds are already gathering at the beginning of the book, world affairs move into prominence. To show how Europe breathed like one huge animal, how everyone's fate was at stake and how each man, down to the lowest functionary, was responsible for the consequences, Sartre judged it best to adopt a technique developed by the American novelist, Dos Passos. This consists in abruptly changing the point of view from person to person. We listen in on a conversation in Paris, on the interior monologue of an old woman in Germany, on the thoughts of a peasant in the south of France, as they take place simultaneously. Sometimes the change is effected within one sentence. The author does not introduce the new setting: the reader must realize from the context of the thoughts into whose mind the author is projecting. Consequently, in the second volume there is more reliance on the stream-of-consciousness. This effect of simultaneity has also been called a cinematographic technique: Sartre focuses on a number of different people in quick succession, like the eye of the camera. As a result, the plot does not progress much as far as the principal characters are concerned.

On Friday, September 23, 1938, Chamberlain was trying to get in touch with Hitler, telling his aides to relay to the Chancellor his wish to negotiate and that war should be avoided at all costs. The wind preceding the storm was sweeping Europe. Maurice, a Communist mechanic, and his wife, Zézette, were visiting Brunet who assured them that the U.S.S.R. would be with the proletariat whatever happened. Milan, a Czech living in the Sudetenland, that part of Czechoslovakia demanded by Hitler, was expecting a pogrom organized by the area's Nazis; Mathieu was tanning himself at Juan-les-Pins on the Riviera, at the summer place of his brother, Jacques; Pierre, a well-to-do young Frenchman, was vacationing with Maud, his mistress, in Morocco and Maud sensed for the first time that he too was afraid. Gomez, an ex-painter, now a general in the Spanish Loyalist army, was spending a few days in Marseilles with his wife and small son. Daniel Sereno was playing the attentive husband's role for his wife Marcelle but was already sick and tired of her. In fact, he was expectantly hoping for war to come. Philippe, a young poet, stepson of a general, was pleading for an appointment with the editor of a pacifist journal. By the end of the day, the government of Czechoslovakia had decided on general mobilization. Milan and his family heard the news on the radio with relief.

On Saturday, the French Republic mobilizes. All those having Form 2 draft cards must report. Mathieu has a Form 2 card. He receives a letter from Boris, who is again with Lola, at Biarritz. Jacques explains to Mathieu that the Czechs are only getting what was coming to them. Pitteaux, editor of the Pacifist, has unexpected visitors: General Lacaze, Mme. Lacaze, and a psychiatrist. Philippe, Mme. Lacaze's son, has disappeared, leaving behind a note in which he indicated that he wanted to become a martyr in the cause of peace. General Lacaze holds Pitteaux responsible for his stepson's behavior. Philippe met Pitteaux a year ago and he has converted the boy to his pacifist ideas. The psychiatrist declares that Pitteaux has been an evil influence on Philippe, who was a disturbed young man anyway, a confirmed onanist.

Pierre, on board a steamer bound for France, is looking for Maud, his mistress. Maud is in the captain's cabin, having a somewhat disappointing sexual experience. Pierre is frightened of the impending war; he needs Maud to soothe him. At last he catches sight of her-she looks besotted. He turns away with disgust. Big Louis, an illiterate herdsman, is held up in Marseilles, his earnings taken away by two seedy characters. Phillipe is visiting a forger to have a false Spanish passport made. Pitteaux has sent him there to get rid of him. Philippe had made a nuisance of himself at the offices of the Pacifist lately, and he would not sleep with Pitteaux. The forger tells him he can pick up the passport next morning. Philippe, who stole ten thousand francs before he left home, puts up at a small hotel where he overhears a conversation in the next room between Maurice, the Communist mechanic, and Zézette. Philippe knocks on their door, intending to convince Maurice that wars are futile. Maurice, who is a French patriot, hits Philippe and throws him out. Crying on his bed, Philippe wonders why no one understands his good intentions. He is a young Rimbaud, he will become a famous poet. Then they will be sorry for the way they acted. He tries to console himself with the thought that his mother must be shedding tears for him. Tonight she would not let General Lacaze sleep with her. He thinks of his mother's lovely arms and goes on weeping.

On Sunday, Daniel goes to Mass. Big Louis tries to get a job lifting casks, but he is told he is a No. 2 and must report at Montpellier. Sarah, Gomez' wife, sees him on the road with a bandage on his head (he was knocked down the previous night when they took his money). He wants Sarah to read his draft card. She affirms that he has to go to Montpellier. She puts a new bandage on his head, gives him some money and advises him not to fight if he can help it.

Boris is dreamily thinking of his future. He has one more year with Lola. Then he will be drafted and he will die in action in 1942, having known only one woman. He reflects that perhaps it suffices to know only one person, if one has known her thoroughly. Pierre is lying in bed on board the steamer; Maud comes to see him; he has thrown up everything in his stomach, now he is vomiting his phlegm. He tells her that he saw her yesterday coming from the captain's cabin. She expects him to start a scene, but he acts in a blase manner, saying that what she does is her business. She realizes that he regards her as a prostitute. She tells him that everything is over between them and leaves contemptuously. The hospital at Berck, in the exposed northeastern corner of France, is being evacuated. One of the invalids, Charles, is dressed by his nurse and is then hurtled onto a freight car with a number of others. On the train he makes the acquaintance of Catherine, a beautiful Austrian girl who has fled from the Nazis. When the train stops, a nurse asks if anyone needs the urinal. At first no one dares to respond, then hands start going up one by one.

Finally, the girl next to Charles asks for it. Charles would like to stop up his ears. The stench is unbearable. But suddenly he feels a sad tenderness toward her, thinking of how humiliated she must be.

Mathieu has dinner with General Gomez, Sarah's husband. Gomez is enjoying the war. At the table, Mathieu feels that he has not earned the food he is taking. Gomez has a right to eat, as a soldier fighting for the good cause. Mathieu has done nothing, the French are doing nothing. Daladier, the French premier, is indignant about the urgent messages Benes is sending him from Czechoslovakia. Boris is sitting in his cafe, estimating the number of omelettes he is likely to consume during his lifetime. Philippe, too, is sitting at a cafe table composing a poem about himself, The Martyr. Then he goes to a night club. Charles' train has arrived at Laroche-Migenne. They remove him from the freight car. He loses sight of Catherine and is afraid he will never see her again; he cries after her, but there is no answer. He curses the people around him, desperately trying to see where she is. Philippe makes the acquaintance of Flossie, a young colored woman at the night club. He goes back to her rooming house with her, drunk, and falls asleep. Flossie has to keep him awake to have him make love to her. Big Louis arrives at the railway station and buys a ticket to Montpellier. He understands nothing about the war. He would like to learn what it is all about; however, no one would talk to him. He gazes at a newspaper, wishing he could decipher the secrets it contains, but he is illiterate. His tears are beginning to flow.

Comment

As Hoederer says in *Dirty Hands,* every one of us is half an accomplice, half a victim. Our responsibility diminishes in the measure as an increasing part of us belongs to the latter category. Big Louis was created as an example of one who is almost purely a victim. It should have been the responsibility of the Third Republic to teach him to read. Almost no one has ever been kind to him; he has been used, taken advantage of and thrown out each time when no longer exploitable. Charles, of course, is, largely speaking, a victim too. With Philippe the question is no longer quite simple; basically, he is a man of good will, but there are traces of bad faith in him. Pitteaux, the editor of the pacifist journal, is clearly on Sartre's blacklist. Pacifism is an evasion of the issues. It is therefore not surprising to find that he has evil designs on Philippe. Mathieu, as always, hesitates and simply lets himself be carried along by the events, trying only to preserve his precious freedom which he interprets not as freedom to act, but as freedom to do nothing.

On September 26, at 8:30 p.m., Hitler delivers a violent speech against Czechoslovakia, in which he calls on Benes to accept his conditions or get ready for war. Everyone all over Europe is glued to the radio. Birnenschatz, a French Jew, listens to it and for the first time a cold flash shoots through his spine. He has always refused to think of himself as a Jew. He is a Frenchman and does not accept any responsibility for Jews as such anywhere else in the world. Mathieu thinks of the war in terms of a disease that cannot be helped. Boris is enthusiastic, thinking of the sense of fraternity he will enjoy at the front. He already faces the war as his war, as a stage all men should go through some time during their lives. Milan Hlinka listens to Hitler's voice in the Sudetenland; his family is struck with fear. Gomez, back in Spain, entertains a spark of hope: this must mean war, the western powers will not swallow this. But Chamberlain looks forward to an appeasement; he hopes to pacify Hitler at the cost of giving in on his demands concerning Czechoslovakia.

On Tuesday, Mathieu is back in Paris. Ivich, at Laon, finds the atmosphere of the parental home too oppressive and takes the train to Paris. Philippe leaves the night club and Flossie and feels that the time has now come for martyrdom. He walks down rue Montmartre and starts shouting, "Down with war?" Irène, the secretary at Pitteaux's office, has spotted and followed him. At last Philippe succeeds in antagonizing the people. Irène fights to rescue him, but in vain. He is trampled on by the mob. Mathieu, passing by, decides that this time he will involve himself. Posing as a detective, he disperses the mob and packs Philippe and Irène into a taxicab. However, it turns out that he has to accompany them, because Philippe tries to escape. They get out in front of a house where there is an empty apartment belonging to some friends of Irène. He helps Philippe to bed and eventually decides to stay and sleeps with Irène.

At six o'clock the next morning, Ivich is at the Eastern Railroad Terminal. Mathieu and Irène discover that Philippe bolted during the night. Ivich goes to Mathieu's apartment, and finds his suitcase. After a few minutes, Mathieu himself appears. Ivich finds that his tone has changed: he speaks matter-of-factly, like a radio announcer. Understanding that Ivich has run away from home, Mathieu wants her to stay at his apartment while he is away in the army. He has already made arrangements to have his teacher's salary paid out to Ivich each month. He shows her around the apartment, giving practical information, hands her a thousand-franc note and departs without showing too much affection. Ivich is deeply hurt. She does not know about the affair with Irène, but gathers that she no longer means as much to Mathieu as she used to. She rips up the banknote and goes over to her boyfriend's hotel. She expects the German planes to strike any minute; she has come to Paris to die in a bombing raid, in his arms. She finds him in bed and declares to him that she is ready to lose her virginity. Irène sees Mathieu off to the railroad station. At the last minute, he tells her his name and they part. Boris slips out of Lola's room while she is sleeping and volunteers for three years. Philippe appears at the recruiting office and admits that he is a deserter, in possession of false papers. Actually, he is not a deserter, not having been called to arms yet, and the possession of a false passport is not an offense, since he has never attempted to use it. They call General Lacaze who wants Philippe kept at the station until he comes to get him. On the train, Mathieu opens a letter that came that morning from Daniel. He is apprised that Daniel has had a conversion, he has embraced the Catholic faith because he has realized he needs the Almighty Lord to look down upon him constantly and thereby to make him truly exist. Mathieu crumples the letter with disgust.

Daladier has promised to make an important statement on the radio. Everyone expects it to be a declaration of war. But it turns out that Daladier cannot make his statement because he has just been called to an important conference in Munich between Chamberlain, Hitler, Mussolini and himself. Hearing the news, Boris is cursing under his breath. He reveals to Lola that he has signed up. General Lacaze comes to the recruiting station and tells Philippe that he has done nothing illegal. In the future, instead of his wife, he is going to attend to Philippe's education. He strikes the boy twice and takes him home.

On the night of the 29th to the 30th of September, the Czechoslovak delegation is called to be informed of the outcome of the Munich pact. Chamberlain and Daladier are there and Mastny reads out the agreement. At the hotel room, Ivich, in bed with her boyfriend, suddenly wants to escape from him but she does not dare move, pretending to be asleep. According to the pact, Reich troops will move into the areas where there is a German majority and an International Commission shall determine the territories in which a plebiscite will be held.

Ivich tries to resist, but her boyfriend overpowers her. Back in Munich, Chamberlain cannot suppress a yawn.

Comment

There is an obvious parallel between the rape of Ivich and the fate awaiting Czechoslovakia. The latter is a helpless country, abandoned by her allies, left to be deflowered by the Nazis. What happens to Ivich serves to underline the injustice done to the Czechs.

The next day, Friday, Big Louis, who is in the Army, is told by a soldier that it is now peace again. Big Louis first refuses to believe it, but, seeing the picture of the smiling Daladier and Hitler in the newspaper, he is convinced. When the sergeant major gives him an order, he tries to explain to him that the war is over. The sergeant major insists and Big Louis now decides that he has had enough (he does not understand the difference between what the newspaper writes and actual demobilization), hits his superior and is in turn overpowered by a number of enlisted men who let him have it. Birnenschatz, who has been arguing with other Jews that one should be simply a French patriot, feels ashamed of himself at seeing how the Czechs were let down. Gomez, knowing that the Republican cause is lost without foreign intervention, on learning the news, clenches his teeth and goes on smoking his pipe. Mathieu thinks of the old life in Paris that is going to recommence now. Milan Hlinka, after all the worries and hopes, after all the harassment by the local Nazis, finally resigns himself to his fate and is only sorry for his child. Ivich hears the news incredulously. Will she now have to stay with this young man whom she hates? Landing at Paris airport, Daladier fears that he is going to be mobbed by indignant Frenchmen. Instead, they greet him with shouts of "Hurrah for peace!" Daladier can hardly believe his ears.

Comment

The Reprieve makes interesting reading, but, on the whole, the camera-eye, simultaneous-exposure technique has more drawbacks than advantages. At certain times, it contributes to the effects that Sartre wishes to achieve: the interconnected nature of civilization, the absurdities involved in our social system, the injustice that is done to people on all levels and all kinds of pretexts. But often the juxtaposition of events seems arbitrary, pointless and scatters and disperses events and individuals to an extent that disturbs the reader and lessens the impact the work might otherwise make. In the next volume, Sartre abandons this technique, as he himself must have doubted that it could be successfully sustained in more than one book.

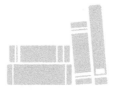

THE ROADS TO FREEDOM

....

PART ONE

The date is June 15, 1940. Ex-General Gomez, now a refugee living in New York City, awakens from a nightmare in which an octopus was sucking his blood. He finds that the octopus was no dream: it is the overpowering, humid heat embracing him. Outside, it is the catastrophic intensity of the light, stronger even than in Spain. He has been copiously perspiring for weeks and he is out of clean shirts. An American friend comes to introduce him to an editor who might employ him as an art critic. The friend tells him that the Governor of Delaware has been received by LaGuardia, that the Giants won yesterday, and, casually, that Paris has fallen to the Germans. Gomez' wife and son were living in Paris the last time he heard. The last Republican resistance is being mopped up in Spain. The friend tells him to keep smiling, otherwise he will never get the job. In France, Sarah Gomez is fleeing from Paris with her son. Her car breaks down and they continue on foot. Gomez is hired and visits the Museum of Modern Art with his friend. But, to his horror, he finds that art no longer means anything to him. The experience of the war has reduced the significance of art as a mode of expression for him. He decides to go to a French restaurant, to see how the French are reacting to the news. He wants to enjoy their grief: he is resentful of France for having given no effective support to the Republicans. But he finds that the bartender is a Canadian. There is only one Frenchman around, an old hairdresser, and Gomez feels too sorry for him to offend him. He ends up by paying for the hairdresser's drinks.

Comment

Sartre's impressions of New York are based on a sidetrip he took there as a newspaper correspondent in 1945.

Somewhere in northeastern France, Mathieu and his battalion have spent the night sleeping in the fields. They have been retreating ever since the beginning of the war without ever having come in contact with the enemy. They know that the armistice is only hours away. They no longer obey their superiors willingly. The past few weeks have wrought subtle changes in their fundamental attitudes. Before, they used to think that they belonged to the greatest nation on earth and it was up to the English or the Germans to apologize for not being completely human, that is, French. Now, they suddenly feel accidental. Nippert and Schwartz, two Alsatians, are beginning to orient themselves toward a new allegiance.

Having been wounded in action and evacuated to Marseilles, Boris Serguine is lying on his hospital bed. A friend of his has offered to fly him to England where they might have a chance to go on fighting the Nazis. Boris wants to wait until Lola comes back from Paris, in two days. Now Ivich comes to fetch him.

Georges, her boyfriend with whom she spent a night in a hotel, married her when it became evident that she was pregnant. She has since had a miscarriage and while her husband is at the front she is living with her in-laws, a very rich and thoroughly upper-middle-class couple. Boris and Ivich go to a cafe. Ivich professes to hate the French because Ivich constantly has to feel ashamed of herself now that France has been defeated. She reveals that she detests the mother-in-law's whole household and would like to live with Boris and Lola. Boris acquiesces and already sees himself as a high school teacher. He is going to marry Lola and will grow old and bald in respectability.

There is a false rumor that the armistice has been signed, but it soon evaporates. Pinette, Mathieu's neighbor, tells him that he is ashamed to go home. His father-in-law was decorated in the First World War. He would like to do at least something before this war is over. A group of drunken French soldiers marches down the road. They invite Mathieu's company to join them on a rampage, but no one moves. They disappear and a few minutes later a Messerschmitt mows them down. Mathieu accompanies Pinette to see a young woman who runs the local post office. At ten thirty p.m. all the commissioned officers of the division, who have been in conference at the general's headquarters, get into their cars and disappear, never to return. The soldiers, dumbfounded, watch them leave. Their procession reminds Mathieu of a cortege of gods returning to Olympus after a sojourn on earth.

Comment

This passage underscores Sartre's contention that the ruling classes of France did not shoulder their responsibilities during the war.

A few miles away, at Épinal, the fighting is still going on. A few stray soldiers cross the village where Mathieu's battalion is quartered; one of them collapses and dies while walking. Pinette hopes that perhaps it is not yet too late for him to participate in the action. But for the moment he goes off with his acquaintance at the post office. The other soldiers have discovered some wine and, abandoned and fearful of the future, they get intoxicated. Mathieu is critical of them, but to show his solidarity he too drinks some wine; however, he is too intellectual to let himself go like the others.

Comment

One of Sartre's recurrent **themes** is the inability of the intellectual to break through the wall that separates him from the masses. The universal fate of the Sartrean hero who is full of good will toward the common man is a lack of comprehension, distrust and malice from the very social class he wishes to succor.

The Germans are entering Paris without resistance. Daniel Sereno, again living alone while Marcelle is at Dax in the Pyrenees, taking care of her baby, is strolling in the deserted city. He feels lighter now that he is not seen by all the pompous-faced bourgeois who are ordinarily milling about on the street. He decides that he is going to like the Germans, as the destroyers of a civilization he hates. On the quai of the Seine, he catches sight of a young man about to drown himself. It is Philippe, General Lacaze's stepson. Philippe had been called to arms and sent to the front. When the Germans attacked, he panicked and ran. He somehow got back to Paris to meet his mother but found no one in the house. Presumably, Mme. Lacaze had fled south before the Germans. Dejected, Philippe intended to commit suicide.

Daniel holds him back just as he is getting ready to jump. At first Philippe wants to fight him off, but Daniel prevails upon him and takes him to his apartment. They have some drinks and Philippe tells his story, disclosing that he has an Oedipus complex. Daniel tries to turn things around, maintaining that it is really his stepfather's opinion Philippe cares about: his mother would have been indulgent to him; he wanted to commit suicide because he failed as a man from General Lacaze's point of view. Daniel offers to liberate Philippe from his stepfather's shadow. He will be Philippe's analyst. After the treatment, he affirms, Philippe should throw him away like a piece of refuse. Actually, Daniel does not look forward to being thrown overboard: he hopes to re-educate and conquer Philippe.

Comment

Evidently, Sartre is here mapping out a new course of action for Daniel as a Nazi collaborator. This was one of the choices open to Frenchmen during the years 1940-44, and Sartre wanted to demonstrate its implications through a principal character in the novel. However, he failed to follow up its development and abandoned the project in the fourth volume.

Pinette leads the post-office employee to the fields. Before she lets him satisfy his desire, however, she is gripped by fear of what is to become of her when the Germans come. Pinette dispels her anxiety for the moment. Charlot, a Jew, worries about his future under the German occupation. The horizon is reddened by the glow of a town that the Germans set fire to because they encountered resistance there. The villagers are apprehensive that perhaps the soldiers quartered with them might try to fight too, but Mathieu's comrades reassure them that they have no intention of doing so. Suddenly, they see a small detachment of well-disciplined soldiers approaching. For a moment they think they are Germans, but they turn out to be French infantrymen, under the command of a lieutenant. They inquire about where the town hall is and go off in the direction indicated. The post-office employee comes to implore Mathieu to prevent Pinette from fighting. In order to escape from her, Pinette leaves the village and secretly returns with Mathieu. He tries to dissuade Pinette, but without much conviction. Pinette chooses a rifle in the school where his comrades are already asleep. He wants to join the lieutenant, who, with his small detachment, is going to fight a rear-guard action against the Germans.

In the last moment, Mathieu takes a rifle too. Mathieu's brother, Jacques, and his wife are driving south escaping from Paris. They want to reach their country home at Juan-les-Pins. Finding no lodgings for the night, they decide to catch some sleep in the car. The lieutenant installs Pinette and Mathieu with three other soldiers on the belfry. His men are holding the school building and the town hall as well. He has locked up Mathieu's comrades in the basement of the town hall and has the civilian population of the village evacuated. The other three soldiers are not particularly impressed by Mathieu and Pinette. They have been fighting a delaying action for the past fifteen days in order to cover the retreat of Mathieur's division. They are seasoned professional soldiers who know what they are doing, and have no time for sentimentality. However, as they begin to talk the ice breaks slowly between them. Mathieu wonders why he is going to die. But suddenly he makes up his mind: he has had enough of the remorse, the reservations, the restrictions that have characterized his life up to now. He accepts no judges and he decides that his death will provide the ultimate sense of his life.

Lola has rejoined Boris at Marseilles. She probably has cancer of the womb, but she will not speak of it. Boris, ignorant of Lola's condition, has everything planned: he will marry her, take a teaching job at Castelmaudary and Ivich will cook for them. Lola realizes the absurdity of this plan and when she learns that Boris has an opportunity to fly to England she urges him to go. She promises that she will take care of Ivich if she cannot live with her in-laws.

A few minutes after six, the battle starts. Mathieu kills a German and feels lighter. But more Germans come; they overrun the town hall and silence the school building too. One by one the other soldiers on the belfry are knocked out of action. Mathieu alone continues to hold out, killing a number of enemy troops. He feels that he is avenging himself. Every shot represents to him the liquidation of one of his past weaknesses: one for Marcelle whom he should have abandoned, one for Odette, Jacques' wife, whom he dared not love, one against every law and commandment, one for man, one for the world and one for virtue. When he dies, he has delayed the German advance by fifteen minutes.

Comment

Though at the end of his life Mathieu realizes his freedom and thereby becomes authentic, Sartre has said that Mathieu did not represent his ideal of the existentialist hero, for his liberty is anarchistic, whereas mankind can only be saved through organized revolution. At any rate, the significance of his last hour is that he now redeems the indecision, the vacillations of a wasted lifetime: he transforms himself into action, erasing every one of his past waverings by an act of self-assertion, the killing of yet another enemy soldier.

PART TWO

After fighting for eight days without interruption, Brunet, the Communist Party functionary, one of the former editors of L'Humanié, realizes that the war is over and lets himself be taken prisoner by the Germans.

When the rank and file lose their masters, they suffer in the spiritual no man's land between two authorities; they seem to lose their human shape in the vacuum. The majority of the French soldiers are relieved when the Germans take charge. They quickly adopt their new bosses, symbolically setting their watches according to Berlin time. In an oblique way, they are already singing the praises of the conqueror; all their remarks are padded with implicit admiration for them. They try to delude themselves into thinking that the Germans are going to be benevolent masters. Brunet attempts to build on the injustices they are exposed to, but the prisoners, like the majority of ordinary Frenchmen, are only too eager to settle for a minimum if they are allowed to continue their humdrum lives and have their little satisfactions.

Brunet makes the acquaintance of Schneider, a leftist intellectual who is nevertheless not connected with the Communist Party. Though a man of great integrity and courage, Schneider identifies himself with the run-of-the-mill Frenchman. A German soldier tosses a few slices of bread over the barbed wire to the famished prisoners, and there is an undignified scuffle. After the incident, Brunet asks Schneider if he too picked up some slices. Schneider claims that he did, but Brunet knows that this is not true; Schneider only does not want to seem better than his fellow prisoners. Brunet and Schneider are packed aboard a train with hundreds of other war prisoners. These men are hoping that, now that the war is over as far as France is concerned, they will be allowed to go home. But the train takes the line leading to Germany. This pleases Brunet, because he knows that he has a much better chance of success among dissatisfied people. He hopes that the objectives for which he has been working right from the beginning of his captivity can now be realized: they will not forget the lesson of their humiliation.

Comment

The third volume is manifestly uneven. The second part reflects Sartre's changing preoccupations. He simply seems to have tired of the principal characters of the novel. He leaves them scattered over the globe and never resumes the threads of their dislocated lives. Indications are that Sartre originally intended to end the cycle on an optimistic note but, in 1948-1949, he again came to the conclusion that humanity was engaged on a course of repression and tyranny. Seeing no place for Mathieu in postwar France, he chose to dispose of him by way of self immolation.

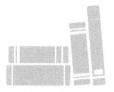

THE ROADS TO FREEDOM

In the prisoner of war camp in Germany, Brunet is more successful in organizing the opposition elements. He helps them fight their daily battles against inadequate rations and unheated barracks. Politically, the party line he adheres to is the official Communist position of the thirties. He professes that the Nazi-Soviet pact of 1939 was mere temporizing and that sooner or later the USSR would join the war against the Axis powers. However, a new comrade arrives, claiming that Russia and Germany have made up for good. Much of Brunet's work is undone, especially as it turns out that Schneider, his best friend, uses a pseudonym. His real name is Vicarios; he is an ex-Communist who bolted the party in protest against the Hitler-Stalin pact. Though Brunet tries to follow the new line, ultimately he sides with Schneider when the latter is subjected to attacks by the prisoners. They attempt to escape together, but the alarm is sounded and Schneider is shot to death. Brunet realizes that the camp commandant has been alerted of their escape by some of his fellow prisoners. He is taken back behind the barbed wire.

Comment

Only excerpts from the fourth volume have been published. They appeared in two consecutive issues of Sartre's journal, *Les Temps modernes* (*Modern Times*), in 1949. During the corresponding period, Sartre sharply condemned some of the methods and tactics used by Stalinism. Ever since 1949, there has been no indication that Sartre wished to finish the cycle.

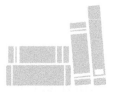

THE ROADS TO FREEDOM

. . . .

MATHIEU DELARUE

The similarities between him and Sartre have often been pointed out. They are of the same age, they have the same profession, they were drafted at the same time. Sartre himself showed a willingness to encourage speculation along these lines. He pointed out in an interview that while he made Mathieu a teacher at the Lycée Buffon, in the first editions of *Age of Reason* he at times inadvertently wrote "Pasteur" instead of "Buffon". Sartre taught at the Lycée Pasteur. Here again, as in *Nausea*, the attentive reader is faced with the somewhat embarrassing evidence that the **protagonist** represents an official, edited version of the author. Mathieu is roughly that part of Jean-Paul that the latter acknowledges in front of the world. To be sure, Mathieu has frailties: mostly, he can be blamed for some of his actions from a purely philosophical point of view. Yet his character is curiously devoid of any suggestion of meanness, envy, vanity or considerations of physical well-being. He is not an existentialist god, but he is a close approximation of a modern saint. He is exclusively a man of good will and his bad faith, if one can call it that, it's of a theoretical nature, never directed toward practical gains. Mathieu's only fault is that he did not translate his freedom into action. His death, however, is a redemption: he avenges his weak moments by as many murders. This was certainly not the way Sartre behaved during the war: unlike Mathieu, he was not an artillery observer but was attached to the Army Medical Corps and it is safe to say that he never used his rifle. This should not be construed as meaning that there was anything ignoble about his Army experience. Sartre has very poor eyesight; his health is fragile. It is merely painful to see him posing as a different physical type. More significantly, Mathieu does not suffer from the ailment that, according to Sartre, is the most essential trait of the human condition: the aspiration and failure of the for-itself to seem like, and be, an in-itself. In a sham world, Mathieu, dark and silent, manly and independent, is a reasonably close facsimile of a for-itself that is at the same time a being-in-itself.

DANIEL SERENO

If, in many ways, Mathieu is the white prince of this novel, Daniel is the black one. This is not to say that, according to the Sartrean barometer of good and evil, he is actually more to blame than most members of the bourgeoisie. But, as a lucid, intelligent, perceptive human being, he makes consistently ignoble choices. Out of pure spite, he refuses to lend Mathieu money; he marries Marcelle for the wrong reasons; he is converted to Catholicism, one of Sartre's anathemas; he is about to become a collaborator when we leave him. He is constantly tormented by his inability to become an in-itself. It has been argued by critics that his malady should be shared by all Sartrean creations, since it is the fundamental truth of human experience as outlined in *Being and Nothingness*. While this accusation is not entirely unfounded, Daniel actually represents a special case, that of the man who tries to solve his existential problems by "founding" himself through establishing his self-identity by means of his reflexive consciousness. Daniel, like Hugo Barine, Baudelaire and Genet, is the man who constantly watches himself.

IVICH SERGUINE

Her chief attraction to Mathieu is her unpredictability. She has a fluttering, almost disembodied freedom that Mathieu would like to seize. Their relationship is unsatisfactory, as are all sexual relations in Sartre's opinion: a person's liberty cannot be conquered; if it could, it would no longer be free. Ivich has several other points in her favor: she is generous, unconventional and sophisticated. She is more or less condemned to be unhappy in life, for she makes great demands on people and cannot suffer mediocrity.

LOLA MONTERO

She is almost a literary commonplace, the energetic, beautiful, aging woman, desperately trying to hold on to her youth. She is willing to fight for Boris if she must, but she will not employ any underhanded methods. For her, the truth of life has been reduced to simple principles. She thinks she understands the world. Her self-assured behavior is based on a mistake, but at least she plays the game unflinchingly and with her cards on the table.

JACQUES DELARUE

Mathieu's brother is the incarnation of middle-class prudence, caution and foresight. One could argue that the virtues Sartre detests in him have made France a prosperous nation. From a Marxist point of view, he is the representative of a class whose historical role has been consummated. But the bitterness with which Sartre reacts to bourgeois failings goes beyond the scope of theory. Sartre is more of a bourgeois rebel than a Marxist.

BORIS SERGUINE AND PHILIPPE LACAZE

They resemble each other, perhaps more than any two unrelated characters should in one single novel. This may be regarded as a limitation of Sartre's inventiveness, though the author was certainly aware of the parallelism, for passages dealing with Boris usually directly follow those on Philippe. Both nineteen, they are described as handsome, with a knack for literary expression, though actually having nothing to say. Both have an Oedipus complex, but neither can find any genuine pleasure in the sexual act. They are young people in the way that the middle-aged Sartre saw the young: somewhat frivolous, vacuous, under the age of reason that Mathieu has attained.

BIG LOUIS (GROS LOUIS)

He is the man chosen by society to pay for us all. A person with a minimum amount of responsibility, he is variously ignored, ridiculed, rejected and punished throughout the book. He is the type Sartre had in mind when he maintained that evil is a projection. His function assigned by society is to be a football. Because we never gave him anything and because he is rejected, he constitutes the perfect target for our contempt and pent-up anger.

BEING AND NOTHINGNESS

INTRODUCTION

This treatise is generally considered to be the author's philosophical chef-d'œuvre. It is undoubtedly the outstanding **exposition** of existential theory in French. Because of its highly technical language and closely-reasoned dialectic, it has been accessible to only a small group of the initiated. The following summary and comments have been designed to give an overall view of Sartre's doctrine, as the philosophy derives from a vision of reality constituting the tenor of the work. The argumentation has been greatly simplified and the terms explained in plain language.

PART ONE - THE PROBLEM OF NOTHINGNESS

Sartre's ontology (study of the structure of being) is based on a duality of matter and consciousness. Inanimate things, he says, have a certain solidity or firmness. A chair, for instance, is entirely a chair in terms of a perfect equation. Nevertheless, matter is unjustified, there is no reason for it to exist. The emergence of consciousness can be explained as an attempt of being (reality to Sartre) to found itself or to justify its own existence. Consciousness, which by itself is not a being in the strict sense, attempts to give a foundation (justification) to things by being always consciousness of something.

Comment

By stating that consciousness is not being in the strict sense, he means that it cannot exist alone. To give a graphic comparison, color is an attribute that cannot exist without an underlying object. Consciousness to Sartre is what color is to material things.

But this attempt at justification must fail, for the only manner in which consciousness may be introduced into matter, which is total density, is by way of nothingness, Consciousness can never be identified with its content, that is, consciousness will always remain a reflection.

Comment

Let us say that I am conscious of a table standing in front of me. Obviously I do not become a table. But even if I am a consciousness-of-a-table there is the underlying texture, so to speak, of consciousness plus the thing I am conscious of. The two can neither be perfectly equated nor separated. That is, consciousness always involves a split that cannot be healed.

Sartre calls matter inanimate things that exist by themselves, in-itself (l'en-soi), while he refers to consciousness as for-itself, (le pour-soi). When I am conscious of something, there is nothing between me and the object of my knowledge. This nothingness dominates Sartre's ontological investigation. Every conscious act: interrogation, destruction, negation, introduces nothingness into the world. Man is the being through whom negativity is injected into the world.

Man is condemned to be what he is not. When we say that this man "is" a student, a politician, or a reactionary, we do not tell the truth. Even when we say that someone "is" angry or "is" in love we state an inaccuracy. The reason for this is that we exist in representation: we are only actors even in the most intimate part of ourselves. In other words, the politician is merely consciousness-of-being-a-politician.

Comment

Sartre's point is not that the person who, for instance, identifies himself as a professor is a "phony" in the usual sense of the word. He may very well have all the necessary qualifications, teach his courses brilliantly, etc. Yet when we talk about a man we cannot reach the same satisfying conclusions as when treating an inanimate object. Man is a subject, which implies that he cannot totally be himself. If he did perfectly coincide with himself, he would be nothing, for consciousness, as we have seen above, cannot exist by itself.

This characteristic of consciousness is exemplified in the phenomenon of bad faith. Bad faith is lying to oneself. The king who tells himself that he is a ruler by some divine sanction is in bad faith. Sincerity is not only impossible, it is a manifestation of bad faith. When we claim to be sincere, we claim to be what we are not, we lie to ourselves, and this is what we call bad faith. As for good faith, here we face the same dilemma: good faith seeks to be an in-itself, which it should be, but cannot be. Though sincerity and good faith are equally hopeless projects, Sartre affirms in a footnote that we can escape from bad faith through authenticity. But he fails to develop the concept of authenticity.

Comment

It is highly significant that Sartre has never defined philosophically how authenticity could exist and in what it would consist. As a matter of fact, if "authentic" is to be taken as genuine or real, it would be very difficult to posit it as a human conduct on the basis of Sartre's ontology. The main thesis of his metaphysics is that man is not genuine and not real. Yet in *Existentialism* he suddenly jumps to the conclusion that good faith indeed exists and he implicitly identifies good faith with authenticity.

PART TWO - BEING FOR-ITSELF

If it is hard to tell the truth about oneself (le soi), it is nevertheless possible to be truthful about myself (le moi). The reason for this is that what Sartre calls myself, the ego or the person (la personne), is constituted exclusively of the past. It is the unifying principle of experience. To the consciousness, the ego appears as a transcendent datum; it has the same relationship to the for-itself as the external world. Thus it can be said simply that the past is an in-itself. The "I" of the psyche is the ego of consciousness and not its self. We have said that it was impossible to say with complete sincerity that "I am happy" or "I am a businessman." But as soon as I pronounce it, this may become true. This is so because consciousness is a for-itself, but, petrifying itself in the past, it becomes an in-itself. One is not what one is but I was what I was.

Here Sartre has found a **metaphysical** formula for a phenomenon that has long fascinated and perplexed poets and writers. They have talked about the turmoil, the liquid and incomprehensible quality of life, contrasting with this the beauty, meaning and picturesqueness of the past. Sartre's explanation is that in the past we become objects, no different from a stone, a table or a book. The past lies there, there is no question about it. In other words, in the past we become endowed with a nature, we were what we were, we attain the stability of matter.

Consciousness is impersonal and unsubstantial. It is a presence, that is, it is present to being in the act of nihilation. What we call the present is precisely this negation of being. It is not what it is (past). This means that the present is the for-itself in its evasion from the past towards the future.

The last definition is salient because it posits man as a project; of the three modes, the future is the most important to Sartre. The for-itself is an evasion or flight towards the future. We are future-oriented. Sartre terms this evasion "transcendence" (la transcendance).

Transcendence as man's future-directedness is a new interpretation of the term, stated by the German phenomenologists. Do not confuse this with the conventional philosophical definition of the transcendent (that which is beyond the senses).

PART THREE - BEING FOR-THE-OTHER

The existence of the "other" (l'autrui), that is, of other men, is revealed, for example, in the sentiment of shame. When I experience it, I am ashamed of myself in front of someone else. Thus shame necessarily posits the existence of another consciousness. The apparition of the other one puts me into the position of judging myself as an object. Shame is recognition; I recognize that I am as others see me. As far as I am concerned, the other is an object. If I see a man pass on the street, Sartre asks, in what way does he differ from all other objects? If he were just another constituent of my visual field, I would class him in the temporospatial order. He would represent just another additional datum. But if I know that he is a man, that is, a consciousness, this causes a disorganization of my field of perception. I am no longer in the center of my universe. The appearance of the other causes the flight of my things towards a term that I perceive as an object but that nevertheless escapes me inasmuch as it unfolds its own organization, its own laws, its own distances around itself.

Comment

How are we to understand Sartre's words? He holds that the essential difference between inanimate objects and humans is that one has no control over the latter. John, passing me on the street, forms certain ideas about me in his mind, which I am incapable of changing. He sees me as he pleases; moreover, he has introduced an entirely new concept into my world. I have recognized that I am not the only center, that things do not only belong to me but to him as well. The other person is another intelligence which forms its own relationships to things, with its own logic: he disintegrates my world.

The Body (*Le Corps*). The body is an in-itself for the other (as far as other people are concerned), and even for me inasmuch as I recognize my objectivity under the gaze of others. I can see myself in a mirror. I can see my hands, etc. In cases like this I perceive myself as others do, i e., I see my otherness, and the being that is revealed to me in such cases is my being for-the-other (l'être-pour-autrui). Inasmuch as it is body-for-the-other, the human body is an in-itself, inasmuch as it exists for the subject, it is pure for itself.

Comment

With this ingenious solution Sartre hopes to give a new dimension to the body-mind relationship. He does not reduce all the body to mind as the idealists; he does not claim, as materialists do, that all psychological phenomena are basically physical. He alleges that they both exist. The body is that by virtue of which the for-itself can exist in the world of extension: it is the for-itself's principle of individuation. To explain what he means, let us take the case of so-called physical pain. When I hurt my finger what I feel is actually a perception "in the brain," as they say, but to localize it is actually meaningless, because I feel the pain in my finger without any consciousness of the perception's being localized in some part of my brain. Thus the body can be reduced to a bundle of perceptions of pain, pleasure, cold, heat, etc., as far as the thinking subject is concerned. That is, from our own point of view, there is nothing material about the body; the only way we know it is through different perceptions; my legs are perceptions of muscle spasms, temperature, blood circulation, etc. There is nothing physical about it. However, as objects for other people, who perceive us from outside, we are purely material. The same way, we can have outside views of ourselves, as when we are looking at some part of our own body or even looking at an X-ray picture of ourselves, and this is what Sartre calls the perception by the subject of his being-for-the-other.

What are one's possible relationships with the other? The first attempt is love: the conquering of the other's freedom. Its corollary is masochism which implies becoming an object for the other. The second attempt, called desire, aims to conquer the other's body, while the third, hatred, represents my wish to liberate myself from the other's presence. Each of these must end in failure, for the other is a subject and I cannot possess him as such.

PART FOUR - HAVING, DOING, AND BEING

The most important doctrine under this heading is that of free will. Actions are, by definition, intentional. This means that accidental consequences, such as fires, collisions, or deaths caused unintentionally are not actions. On the other hand, the executioner who has been given the order to kill and carries it out has acted. No state of fact whatever can cause human action. An action is the projection of the for-itself towards that which is not and which is not cannot determine what is. The past by itself cannot determine an action. There are no actions without motives, but this is not to be understood in the same sense as when we legitimately say that there is no result without a cause.

To take an example, fear is a so-called motive. Someone is afraid of dying of hunger. But this fear is senseless unless we suppose that life is valuable. Fear depends on the value one attaches to life, it refers to a system of values. Emotions do not determine actions. What happens when I assert that I am happy is that I affect myself with happiness as a magic recourse in the face of a crucial situation. To be happy implies first to make oneself happy. Emotion is no "physiological storm;" it is a conduct one chooses to attain a certain end. My fear is free and is a manifestation of my freedom. We choose to be fearful in certain situations. Similarly, being ambitious, cowardly, or angry simply means conducting oneself in such and such a manner.

Comment

Let us suppose that John is terrified during an examination for which he is ill-prepared. He knows that he must pass it if he wants to get into medical school. Long ago he has made up his mind to become a physician and would consider himself a failure for the rest of his life in any other profession. This is the scale of values he has chosen. In its light, the examination is of the greatest moment. In fact, so much depends on it that he prefers to choose an emotional commitment rather than a rational solution.

What are some of the roads open to him? He may decide to be angry with the teacher; or he may affect himself with disdain; he may move himself to pity for his own lot; mother's poor innocent child ruined by the heartless professor; etc. He has opted for fear as a magic recourse in this difficult situation. It is "magic" because it thrusts reason aside. An argument in favor of this theory is that when something crucial happens to us we in fact do go through a whole gamut of different emotions. A person who has been given a harsh sentence may alternate between bursts of anger and tears; Sartre would claim that he is testing the efficacy of various modes of conduct.

Under the name of facticity (la facticité), Sartre catalogues the limits of freedom. Crude reality can limit our freedom of action, but freedom establishes the framework in which things will manifest themselves as limits. If, for instance, a rock proves too heavy to put into one's pocket, it is only that we originally conceived of it as capable of being put into a pocket. To be free is not equivalent to being able to do what one wants. Freedom does not entail success. In common usage, freedom implies the realization of some project. Its philosophical concept means only autonomy of choice. Without limits, that is to say, without a framework of possibilities, the term "freedom" would be devoid of sense. The main categories of facticity are the following: My position is the result of my conception of the world. In itself it is neutral. Only my projection towards a certain aim makes of it an obstacle or an aid. My past is there, but I choose its sense. My neighbor restricts me by his presence, but this only implies that freedom is limited by freedom. Finally, death has no relation to my being as a for-itself, only the other is mortal.

Comment

Death in fact is meaningless to the individual. Either one believes in an afterlife, and then there is of course no death, or one does not. In the second case a little reflection will show that the terms "life" and "death" are contradictory. All one can experience is life, death is an absence of experience, therefore it has no reality. There is no time when I could legitimately assert, "I am dead." If I said it, it would be a lie and as soon as I could truthfully say it, the "I" would no longer be there. Other people die, but I cannot die. There exists fear of death, which I learn from experiencing from outside the death of others.

Existential Psychoanalysis

This is one of the subtitles in Part Four of *Being and Nothingness*. Its point of departure is bad faith, just as the point of departure of Freudian psychoanalysis is the unconscious. Sartre claims that the postulate of the unconscious avoids the difficulties contained in the concept of lying to oneself, which occurs in bad faith. Instead, Freud cuts the individual into two distinct parts, one being the deceiver, the other, the one deceived. The analyst plays a role as a kind of mediator between my unconscious and my consciousness. That is, it predicates an act of lying without a liar. But, Sartre points out, Freud registers resistance on the part of the patient when the analyst begins to approach the truth. What is it in the patient that resists? If his tendencies were truly unconscious, he would be there as an impartial witness. In other words, the censor must be familiar with that which it suppresses. How would the censor know which impulses must be suppressed if it were not aware of these impulses? The censor is conscious of itself, which means that it is in bad faith. Therefore, existential psychoanalysis rejects the postulate of the unconscious. Yet, there is a difference between consciousness and knowledge. An existentialist psychoanalyst is needed to explicate to the patient the choices by which he is creating himself.

The objective of man's quest is being. He wants to fuse in himself object and subject, thereby giving contingent matter a foundation, a justification. This is equivalent to asserting that man's aim is to be God. But the idea of God is contradictory and consequently man exhausts himself in a passion that finally proves useless.

CRITICAL COMMENTARY ON BEING AND NOTHINGNESS

Among the more incisive critics of Sartrean ontology the names of Gilbert Varet, Wilfrid Desan, H. Marcuse, M. A. Natanson, and Jean Wahl should be mentioned. Unfortunately, most critics either had an axe to grind or made their judgments on the basis of a cursory acquaintance with their subject matter. We shall offer the following considerations about the basic problems that emerge from a study of this work; some of them have already been outlined by critics.

Nothingness

Sartre's treatment of this concept is based on a sophism: he speaks of nothing as if it were something. Once the reader concedes him this point, Sartre can lead him on as he pleases. Nothingness simply does not exist.

Man Is Not What He Is

This assertion is obviously irrational. The most fundamental philosophical axiom, the principle of self-identity, states that everything is what it is. Sartre believes that rationalism cannot adequately explain reality. But his book attempts to rationally prove the irrational in man. Many modern philosophers would say that this is impossible.

Human Nature And The Ego Exist Only In The Past

The contention that the ego is no part of consciousness is highly original, but it cannot be argued consistently. Wilfrid Desan's

Tragic Finale discusses this aspect of Sartre's philosophy quite adequately. The ego is a necessary assumption as a unifying link of representations. While the claim that body and mind are one and the same thing, only from two different points of view, might be consistently defended, it contradicts much of the rest of Sartrean dogma. If it were true, then objectively there would be a human nature and man would be determined. Sartre tries to avoid this pitfall by saying that the body of the other is essentially past. But, some might object, this is a very artificial argument.

Free Will Versus Determinism

This constitutes a mystery that no amount of dialectic has been able to clear up so far. On the one hand, reason tells us that there must be a sufficient reason for every result. There are only two things that could explain a man's actions, heredity or environment. To suppose that anything else can affect action would seem irrational. Yet everyone has the direct evidence of his freedom: life would be impossible if we assumed that everything is determined. It is little wonder that Sartre has not been able to tackle this question adequately. Maintaining that a man trapped in a cage with a roaring lion has a choice between various emotional solutions of his problem is manifestly a difficult task. To talk of freedom in the case of a man tied down to a chair and being tortured by the Gestapo is likewise an arduous undertaking. When Sartre discusses the framework in which freedom moves, it becomes evident that either we have to restrict the significance of the term "absolute freedom" so that it will no longer denote what it seems to denote or we have to admit that man's freedom is not absolute. In fact, if the other restricts my freedom by his very presence, it is of little consolation to me that my freedom is only limited by another freedom. The guard who blocks my way when I am trying to walk out of jail restricts my freedom.

The Unconscious

Its existence may be a postulate, but a necessary one. Everything that is not contained in my consciousness at any particular moment but can be recalled into it by means of my memory is unconscious, i.e., John may not be at present conscious of the fact that he was born in 1939, that his brother's name is Francis, that he had an A in biology five years ago. These facts can be remembered if he so chooses. Whether repression takes place the way Freud thought is another matter. On this point many psychologists feel that Sartre is closer to the truth than the Viennese doctor. Binswanger, Medard Boss, Roland Kuhn, and Van Den Berg are names associated with the theory of existential psychoanalysis as related to Sartre's doctrine.

EXISTENTIALISM

....

INTRODUCTION

This pamphlet was originally given by Sartre as a lecture. Conceived at a time when existentialism had just succeeded in extending its appeal to a wider public, it was designed to present Sartre's main doctrines in a nutshell and in a form comprehensible to those without a solid philosophical background. As *Existentialism* is not on a highly technical level, it has often been attacked by critics, for whom it represented a particularly invidious type of vulgarization from the pen of a professional philosopher. However, it is useful for the student who seeks a secure grasp of the coordinating points in Sartrean theory.

Note. The subdivisions here given do not correspond to any in the pamphlet. The original has no headings or divisions. We added them to facilitate the student's work.

SCHOOLS OF EXISTENTIALISM

There are principally two: Christian, among whose adherents he mentions Jaspers, (a German philosopher), and Gabriel Marcel (a French Catholic thinker), and atheistic, among whom he includes Heidegger (the leading exponent of the school in Germany), the majority of French existentialists and himself.

BASIC DEFINITION OF THE TERM "EXISTENTIALISM"

Existence precedes essence. How is this to be understood? With all man made objects, it is essence that precedes existence. For example, in order to make a table the artisan must first have a conception of what he is going to fabricate, (essence), and then he can carry it into execution, giving existence to the idea. Man is not like this. He comes into the world existent but without a nature, without essence. He defines himself while existing, that is, man, and man alone, creates his own essence. He is what he makes himself. Man is his life.

RESPONSIBILITY (LA RESPONSABILITÉ)

If one affirms that man creates or chooses himself, this means that he is responsible. He is not responsible for his own individuality alone, but for all mankind, for, in choosing ourselves, we are choosing mankind. With every one of our actions, we are not choosing merely ourselves, but, implicitly, everyone else, because in our actions we create a certain image of man. We affirm that such and such an act is within the realm of human behavior. (E.g., by eliminating millions of people in gas chambers, the Nazis have added to the concept of man as a historical phenomenon.)

Subjectively, there is no evil conduct: we choose one thing over another because we hope to gain some good. Murdering an innocent man is therefore an implicit affirmation that murder is permissible, it is a good to be striven for. This is what is meant by responsibility.

ANGUISH (L'ANGOISSE)

The man who realizes that in every one of his acts he is responsible for all mankind experiences the phenomenon of existential anguish.

BAD FAITH (LA MAUVAISE FOI)

Not all people seem to be subject to anguish. There are men who mask their anguish in front of themselves, who flee from it. Bad faith is lying to oneself. It is a lie indulged in to avoid human responsibility.

ABANDONMENT (LE DÉLAISSEMENT)

It is the realization that God does not exist. This implies that there is no a priori criterion (God given measure) of good and evil. One chooses one's own values.

DESPAIR (LE DÉSESPOIR)

We must count only on what depends on our will. As man is free, one cannot foretell the future. I can hope that a certain state of affairs will come about at some future period. But all I am sure of is my own individual will; my own capacity to change the world.

SUBJECTIVISM

The existentialist believes in subjectivity because he needs one point of absolute certainty, one axiom upon which to build his theories, and this is provided by the Cartesian formula of "I think, therefore I am." As a subjectivism, existentialism affirms human dignity. It regards man as a subject, whereas materialism conceives of him as an object.

INTER-SUBJECTIVITY

Existentialism does not, nevertheless, stop at the Cartesian cogito. It claims that in the act of reflection implied by "I think, therefore I am" man does not only reach himself alone but himself in the face of others. I am what I am always in relation to others.

THE HUMAN SITUATION OR CONDITION

By this is meant the terms imposed upon me by the existing socioeconomic, physical, physiological factors. The situation does not limit my freedom but rather provides me with the framework within which my freedom can unfold. Freedom does not imply the capacity to do anything one likes. Without conditions, "freedom" itself would be a word devoid for signification.

GOOD FAITH OR AUTHENTICITY (LA BONNE FOI, L'AUTHENTICITÉ)

The actions of men of good faith are always directed toward freedom as their ultimate significance. The authentic person is the one who recognizes his total freedom and the consequences it entails.

TYPES OF ERRONEOUS CONDUCT

There exist two of these, both being manifestations of bad faith (see above):

(a) Cowardice (la lâcheté). Those affected by this hide their total liberty from themselves with deterministic excuses. E. g., Sartre would call a person who blames his failure in later life on his lack of opportunities a child, a coward.

(b) That exemplified by the behavior of "skunks" (salauds). They try to prove that their very existence was necessary. These are people who feel completely at home in the world, telling themselves that they deserve everything they get, that they are indispensable and irreplaceable. The behavior of leaders is often marked by this deceit.

EXISTENTIALIST HUMANISM

Man is, on the one hand, a project, on the other hand, a subjective being present in a human universe (see Inter-subjectivity). These notions are at the basis of Sartrean humanism. It reminds man that he is his only legislator and that he must choose himself in solitude and warns him that he can only realize himself by finding outside of himself the particular aims leading to his liberation.

Comment

In *Existentialism*, Sartre intended to appeal to the general public while refuting some of the accusations leveled against him by critics and philosophers in other camps. The work therefore smacks of propaganda. It contains numerous deviations from Sartre's ontology as expressed in his philosophical works, probably in order to make his ideas more palatable to readers. But some of these differences may be attributed to modifications in his thinking since the publication of *Being and Nothingness*. The first glaring change is the stress on responsibility. There was little mention of this in his previous writings. But now he introduces the social **theme**, the theme of loyalty and interdependence even into the notions of abandonment and anguish. Another modification, fundamental to this particular work, is his attitude toward humanism. We have seen that *Nausea* contains a vehement indictment of humanists. He now claims that what he condemned there and in one of his short stories, "Érostratus," was nineteenth-century humanism, a false, hypocritical concept. Yet no amount of dialectic legerdemain can conjure away the distaste for mankind, keenly felt and metaphysically underpinned, that permeates the bulk of his production prior to 1945. A third important modification concerns the notion of authenticity. Sartre here equates authenticity with good faith, while in *Being and Nothingness* he claimed that these differed from each other and that good faith was impossible to achieve. In fact the entire message of *Being and Nothingness* would seem to exclude the possibility of good faith.

We shall call the attention of the student interested in philosophy to a serious flaw in Sartre's reasoning. He defines man in two ways; as the totality of his acts, and as a project. The first is an objective definition, taken from outside, and conceives of man as the sum total of the imprints he has made on reality, the changes he has brought about in the external world. In this sense we would say that the architect who designed the George Washington bridge becomes a reality in his creation or that the mason who built a house actually comes alive in that structure, for by themselves they are nothing. The second definition, man is a project, is subjective. It essentially concerns itself with the future, and from inside. It says that man is a reaching-into-the-future. Thus, the two definitions are contradictory, for the one defines man in terms of the past, the other, in terms of the future.

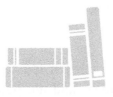

Question: Is Sartre a writer who has dabbled in metaphysics or is he a professional philosopher who writes fiction in order to illustrate his theses?

Answer: On the whole, he is more a writer than a philosopher. He has had excellent training in philosophy, has read widely and is cognizant of the latest trends in the subject. He possesses great acumen and extraordinary lucidity. Yet his point of departure is rather emotional than intellectual. Robert Grimsley, in his *Existentialist Thought*, suggests that Sartre's conception may rest upon pre-cognitive premises. He relies on intuition more than induction or deduction; at any rate, he uses reasoning as a means to justify a certain intuitive conviction, explain an affective state or defend an emotional commitment. Sartre has said of Genet that "his victory is a verbal one." There is much in Sartre's own work to vindicate such a statement. He is a terminological wizard, he coins phrases with uncanny skill, but careful scrutiny shows that the words often hide a shallow idea. In a deeper sense, too, he tries to conjure away reality by insisting on the concept of nothingness, but his conclusions are based on verbal trickery. To be sure, philosophy admits of more than one definition, but those who call Sartre's credentials to question have grounds for their claim.

On the other hand, the critics who, conversely, dismiss Sartre's fiction, contending that it is too abstract or lifeless because it deals with ideas and not people, do not appear to have a very good case. Sartre's fiction is not **didactic** in a sense that esthetes usually condemn in literature. Sartre never argues or explains in his narrative or dramatic pieces, he only shows implicitly and lets the facts speak for themselves. His technique entirely dispenses with the function of the omniscient narrator, and he has increasingly used the stream-of-consciousness method. Ideas are a very real part of the lives of many people. We should not condemn Sartre because he portrays intellectuals. Yet whether he possesses the writer's ability to make his characters convincing is a question that can be answered only by the individual reader. The fact that his production has enjoyed considerable popularity indicates that he does indeed possess this ability.

Question: Show in Sartre's works the **theme** of man attempting to recapture his essence by means of introspection and outline the conceptual background of this theme.

Answer: Examples of this conduct abound in Sartre's fiction and criticism. It is par excellence the sickness he attributes to intellectuals. His study, Baudelaire, devoted to the great nineteenth-century poet, the precursor of symbolism, analyzes this attitude in greatest detail. Baudelaire is constantly watching over his own shoulder, Sartre affirms. He is like Narcissus, absorbed in his reflection; he can never forget himself; he watches himself in the act of seeing and watches in order to see himself looking. He wants to discover who he is, because he is proudly convinced that he is different from other people. Can he find anything, when he turns the spotlight of his intelligence inside? No, Sartre claims, such a search yields nothing, for there is no human nature; consciousness must contain something other than itself if it is to be grasped. Thus Baudelaire's life will be a sterile assertion of his otherness, with the inevitable incapacity for action of the man who incessantly contemplates himself. Lucien Fleurier, in the "Childhood of a Leader", tries to explore his own nature by introspection and fails; his solution will be to create a constant image of himself in other people's minds. Daniel, one of the chief characters in *The Roads to Freedom*, has chosen to be a homosexual to defy society. He too constantly fixes his attention on his self and does not succeed in finding the distinguishing trait that separates him from the rest of mankind which he rejects. Is this idea completely new? No, the conclusion that introspection is unreliable or downright impossible was one of the factors that gave impetus to the development of modern experimental psychology. In French philosophy this trend has been associated with positivism and its founder, Auguste Comte, who contended that while sensory perceptions, physical sensations, pain and pleasure, and even to some extend emotions could be introspectively ascertained, cognition (the thought process) was not accessible to introspection. The brain, Comte argued, is centrally organized; you cannot split yourself in two parts, one the examiner and the other, the thing examined. With affective states, this attempt is not totally unsuccessful, because the seats of the emotions and of intellection are somewhat separated. The behaviorists (a modern American school) went so far as to exclude the concept of consciousness from their theory. Parenthetically, proponents of introspection answer Comte's argument by admitting that while simultaneous self-reflection on the cognitive level may indeed of impossible, retrospective self-examination can scrutinize the data of consciousness after their occurrence.

It is interesting to note how widely Sartrean conclusions differ from those that experimental psychology draws from the same premise. Sartre sees it as proving the absence of any human nature, while many psychologists have used it to show that man must be studied objectively.

Question: Does Sartrean philosophy represent the triumph of foggy German metaphysics over Gallic lucidity?

Answer: Sartre's paternal grandfather, Professor Schweitzer, was German. Sartre reads German well. Phenomenology, the philosophical trend that has influenced him most profoundly, is a German discipline, and his existentialism itself partly derives from Heidegger. His dialectic at times possesses the characteristically German gift for putting what is clear and simple in such intricate and involuted ways that is becomes well-nigh impossible to comprehend. Another Teutonic quality is Sartre's preference for abstracting notions until they have been completely stripped of all meaning and then juggle with them. His irrationalism may in large measure be traced back to German romanticism; his insistence on the will bears clear indications of Schopenhauer's voluntarism.

A dwindling detachment of French critics is still fighting a rearguard action against everything that has happened to French culture; since the beginning of the nineteenth century. They hold that classicism reflected the true French spirit and ascribe all the evils that have corrupted the texture of their country's civilization to barbaric northern influences. Their dean was the late Julien Benda who, at the age of eighty, still produced a book, Tradition de l'existentialisme, invoking his parting curses on the latest idols of a misguided French populace.

On the other hand, there is much in Sartre that is unmistakably French in the sense of the old tradition. His intuitive understanding, his stress on moral questions, his compassion, his sparkling wit associate him with the best qualities of the French heritage.

Question: Is Sartre a humanist?

Answer: The answer is a qualified yes. Though he denounced humanists in two of his fictional works, *Nausea* and "Érostratus," in no uncertain terms, in *Existentialism* Sartre turned around to claim that he was himself one. However, he maintained that his brand of humanism was a bird of a different feather. It differs, he stated, from classical humanism where man is regarded as an end. Existentialist humanism, he says, deserves its name because it teaches man that he is his sole legislator and that he has to reach outside himself in order to liberate and realize himself. Like so many other Sartrean statements, this one, too, approximates a play on words: existentialism does not consider man an end, because man is a project. What he means is that man is a beginning, not an end. But "end" in this definition is actually equivalent to "ultimate value", and Sartre implicitly agrees that man is the ultimate value (we are using the term value here in its non-technical sense), since he is an atheist and proclaims that we live in a human universe. Sartre contends that we are means to each other in the realization of our projects; nevertheless, we are all responsible, for society is interrelated and by choosing ourselves we are choosing mankind. In other words, according to both classic and existentialist humanism, man is the ultimate value, but for the latter this means the individual, not an abstract notion of humanity. Sartrean humanism carries within it a seed of self-destruction: you cannot be the supporter of the individual without recognizing the rights of society as a whole.

BIBLIOGRAPHY

WORKS BY SARTRE

Theatre

Les Mouches (Paris: Gallimard, 1943). Trans.: *The Flies* (New York: Knopf, 1947).

Huis-Clos (Paris: Gallimard, 1944). Trans.: *No Exit* (New York: Knopf, 1947).

Morts sans sépulture (Paris: Gallimard, 1946). Trans.: *The Victors: Three Plays* (New York: Knopf, 1949).

La Putain respectueuse (Paris: Nagel, 1946). Trans.: *The Respectful Prostitute*, Art and Action (New York: Twice A Year Press, 1949).

Les Mains Sales (Paris: Gallimard, 1948). Trans.: *Dirty Hands: Three Plays* (New York: Knopf, 1949).

Le Diable et le bon Dieu (Paris: Gallimard, 1951). Trans.: *The Devil and the Good Lord and Two Other Plays* (New York: Knopf, 1960).

Nekrassov (Paris: Gallimard, 1955). Trans: *Nekrassov* (London: Hamish Hamilton, 1956).

Les Séquestrés d'Altona (Paris: Gallimard, 1960). Trans.: *The Condemned of Altona* (New York: Knopf, 1961).

Novels And Short Stories

La Nausée (Paris: Gallimard, 1938) Trans.: *Nausea*, (New York: New Directions, 1949).

Les Chemins de la liberté: I, L'Age de raison (Paris: Gallimard, 1945). Trans.: *The Roads to Freedom*: I, *The Age of Reason* (New York: Knopf, 1947). II, *Le Sursis* (Paris: Gallimard, 1945). Trans.: II, *The Reprieve* (New York: Knopf, 1947). III, *La Mort dans l'âme* (Paris: Gallimard, 1949). Trans.: III, *Troubled Sleep* (New York: Knopf, 1951). IV, *La dernière chance* (excerpts published in *Les temps modernes*, November and December, 1949). Untranslated.

Le Mur (Paris: Gallimard, 1939). Trans.: *The Wall and Other Stories* (New York: New Directions, 1948).

Philosophy

L'Imagination (Paris: Presses Universitaires, 1936). Trans.: *Psychology and Imagination* (New York: Philosophical Library, 1948).

Esquisse d'une théorie des émotions (Paris: Hermann, 1939). Trans.: *The Emotions, Outline of a Theory* (New York: Philosophical Library, 1948).

L'Imaginaire, psychologie phénoménologique de l'imagination (Paris: Gallimard, 1940). Trans.: *The Psychology of the Imagination* (New York: Rider, 1951).

L'Être et le néant (Paris: Gallimard, 1943). Trans.: *Being and Nothingness* (New York: Philosophical Library, 1956).

L'Existentialisme est un humanisme (Paris: Nagel, 1946). Trans.: *Existentialism* (New York: Philosophical Library, 1947).

Critique de la raison dialectique, I; Questions de méthode (Paris: Gallimard, 1960). Partially translated in *Search for a Method* (New York: Braziller, 1963).

Literary Criticism And Other

Situations I, II, III, (Paris: Gallimard, 1947, 1948, 1949). Some of the essays contained in these three volumes have been translated in: Literary and Philosophical Essays (New York: Philosophical Library, 1957).

Baudelaire (Paris: Gallimard, 1947). Trans.: *Baudelaire* (Norfolk: New Directions, 1950).

Saint Genet: comédien et martyr (Paris: Gallimard, 1952). Trans.: *Saint Genet* (New York: Knopf, 1963).

Réflections sur la question juive (Paris: Gallimard, 1954; originally published in 1946). Trans.: *Anti-Semite and Jew* (New York: Shoeken, 1948).

Les Mots (Paris: Gallimard, 1964). Trans.: *The Words* (New York: Knopf, 1964).

WORKS ON SARTRE

Albérès, René Marill. *Jean-Paul Sartre* (Paris: Editions Universitaires, no date). Trans.: *Jean-Paul Sartre: Philosopher Without Faith* (New York: Philosophical Library, 1961). Albérès is one of the most outstanding critics of contemporary literature. This short book serves as a good general introduction.

Beigbeder, Marc. *L'homme Sartre* (Paris: Bordas, 1947). Untranslated. Biographical in approach. Somewhat outdated. Valuable only if used in conjunction with other sources.

Bentley, Eric. *The Playwright as Thinker* (New York: Noonday Press, 1955). A study of Sartre's theater, restricted to an analysis of the early plays.

Campbell, Robert. *Sartre ou une littérature philosophique* (Paris: Ardent, 1945). Untranslated. Incisive study of the relationships of Sartrean thought and fiction.

Champigny, Robert. *Stages on Sartre's Way* (Bloomington: Indiana University Press, 1959). Stresses the esthetic aspect of Sartre's works.

Desan, Wilfrid. *The Tragic Finale* (Cambridge: Harvard University Press, 1954.) An **exposition** and critique of *Being and Nothingness*. The author is mainly conversant with scholastic philosophy.

Jeanson, Francis. *Sartre par lui-meme* (Paris: Seuil, 1955). Jeanson closely collaborates with Sartre. His interpretations are therefore valid from Sartre's point of view. The volume contains excerpts from Sartre's works and many interesting photographs.

Kern, Edith. ed. *Sartre: A Collection of Critical Essays* (Englewood Cliffs: Prentice Hall, 1962). Includes some stimulating pieces as well as some less well informed.

Laing, R. D. and D. G. Cooper. *Reason and Violence: A Decade of Sartre's Philosophy, 1950-1960* (London: Tavistock, 1964). A condensation of *Saint Genet,* the *Critique of Dialectical Reasoning*, and *Search for a Method.*

Magny, Claude Edmonde. *Les Sandales d'Émpedocle* (Neufchatel: La Baconniere, 1945) Untranslated. Contains an interesting analysis of *Nausea.*

Thody, Philip. *Jean-Paul Sartre* (London: Hamish Hamilton, 1960). A comprehensive, conscientious introduction for the general public.

Lightning Source UK Ltd.
Milton Keynes UK
UKHW021604260721
387787UK00011B/2412

9 781645 422648